Mac OS X
Pocket Reference

Mac OS X
Pocket Reference

Chuck Toporek

O'REILLY®

Beijing · Cambridge · Farnham · Köln · Paris · Sebastopol · Taipei · Tokyo

Mac OS X Pocket Reference

by Chuck Toporek

Copyright © 2002 O'Reilly & Associates, Inc. All rights reserved.
Printed in the United States of America.

Published by O'Reilly & Associates, Inc., 1005 Gravenstein Highway North,
Sebastopol, CA 95472.

O'Reilly & Associates books may be purchased for educational,
business, or sales promotional use. Online editions are also available
for most titles (*safari.oreilly.com*). For more information, contact our
corporate/institutional sales department: (800) 998-9938 or
corporate@oreilly.com.

Editor:	Chuck Toporek
Production Editor:	Jeffrey Holcomb
Cover Designer:	Emma Colby
Interior Designer:	David Futato

Printing History:

May 2002:	First Edition.

0-596-00346-3
[C]

Contents

Part III. System Tools

Part IV. Mac OS X Unix Basics

Part V. Task and Setting Index

Mac OS X Pocket Reference

Introduction

This Pocket Reference is intended to be a quick reference guide to Mac OS X. If you're an experienced user, this book may be the only one you'll need. For Mac users who are coming to Mac OS X from earlier versions of the Mac OS, some of the material in this book can serve as a refresher, reminding you how to do certain things that you've always been able to do on the Mac. In addition, you'll also learn more about the Unix side of Mac OS X. For Unix, Linux, or FreeBSD users coming to the Mac for the first time, you'll get a quick summary of how to use Mac OS X's interface and how to use its Terminal application for issuing Unix commands. For Windows expatriates, the Terminal and Unix commands will be all new, but not all too far off from the DOS prompt you've used in the past.

Conventions Used in This Book

The following typographical conventions are used in this book:

Italic

> Used to indicate new terms, URLs, filenames, file extensions, directories, commands and options, program names, and to highlight comments in examples. For example, a path in the filesystem will appear as */Applications/Utilities*.

Constant Width

> Used to show the contents of files or the output from commands.

Constant Width Bold

> Used in examples and tables to show commands or other text that should be typed literally by the user.

Constant Width Italic

> Used in examples and tables to show text that should be replaced with user-supplied values.

Variable Lists

> The variable lists throughout this book present tasks as the answer to a "How do I…" question (e.g., "How do I change the color depth of my display?").

Menus/Navigation

> Menus and their options are referred to in the text as File → Open, Edit → Copy, etc. Arrows will also be used to signify a navigation path when using window options; for example, System Preferences → Login → Login Items means that you would launch System Preferences, click the icon for the Login control panel, and select the Login Items pane within that panel.

Pathnames

> Pathnames are used to show the location of a file or application in the filesystem. Directories (or *folders* for Mac and Windows users) are separated by a forward slash. For example, if you see something like, "…launch the Terminal application (*/Applications/Utilities*)" in the text, that means the Terminal application can be found in the *Utilities* subfolder of the *Applications* folder.

↵

> A carriage return (↵) at the end of a line of code is used to denote an unnatural line break; that is, you should not enter these as two lines of code, but as one continuous line. Multiple lines are used in these cases due to printing constraints.

%, #

The percent sign (%) is used in some examples to show the user prompt for the *tcsh* shell; the hash mark (#) is the prompt for the *root* user.

NOTE

Indicates a tip, suggestion, or general note.

WARNING

Indicates a warning or caution.

Menu Symbols

When looking at the menus for any application, you will see some symbols associated with keyboard shortcuts for a particular command. For example, to open a document in Microsoft Word, you could go to the File menu and select Open (File → Open), or you could issue the keyboard shortcut, ⌘-O.

Figure 1 shows the symbols used in the various menus to denote a keyboard shortcut.

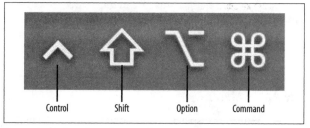

Figure 1. Keyboard accelerators for issuing commands

Rarely will you see the Control symbol used as a menu command option; it's more often used in association with mouse clicks or for working with the *tcsh* shell.

PART I

Mac OS X Survival Guide

The first part of this book is intended to show those who are new to Mac OS X how to acclimate quickly to their new environment. For Windows and Unix users who are coming to Mac OS X, most everything will be new, while Mac OS users will have to adjust the most to relearn the Mac.

This part of the book will cover:

- Changes to Mac OS X from Mac OS 9
- Tips for Windows and Unix users who are new to Mac OS X

Changes to Mac OS X from Mac OS 9

There are many noticeable changes in the user interface from earlier versions of the Mac OS to Mac OS X, while others may not be so apparent. Two of the biggest changes from Mac OS 9 to Mac OS X can be found in the Apple menu and the Control Panels.

The Apple Menu

The Apple menu, displayed as an apple symbol (🍎) in the menu bar, is completely different; you can no longer store aliases for files, folders, or applications there. Here's what you'll find in Mac OS X's Apple menu:

About This Mac

This option will only tell you information about your Mac. In earlier versions of the Mac OS, the About box would change depending on which application was active. For information about the application, you now have to use the application menu (located to the right of the Apple menu) and select the About option.

Get Mac OS X Software

Selecting this option will take you to Apple's Mac OS X software page (*http://www.apple.com/downloads/macosx/*) in your default web browser.

System Preferences

System Preferences replaces most of the Control Panels from earlier versions of the Mac OS. See the "System Preferences" section later in this book for more details.

Dock

This menu offers a quick way to change settings for the Dock (described later).

Location

This is similar to the Location Manager Control Panel from earlier versions of the Mac OS; it allows you to change locations quickly for connecting to a network and/or the Internet.

Recent Items

This menu option combines the Recent Applications and Recent Documents options from Mac OS 9's Apple menu into one convenient menu. A Clear option allows you to reset the recent items from the menu.

Force Quit

Thanks to Mac OS X's protected memory, you don't have to restart the entire system if an application crashes or freezes. Instead, you can come here (or use Option-⌘-Esc) to open a window that lists the applications running on your system. To Force Quit a stuck application, simply click on the application name, then click on Force Quit.

Sleep

Selecting this option will automatically put your Mac into sleep mode. This is different from the settings you dictate in System Preferences → Energy Saver for auto-sleep functionality. To "wake" your computer from sleep mode, simply press any key.

Restart

This will restart your Mac. If any applications are running, they will be automatically shut down, and you will be prompted to save changes for any files that were open.

Shutdown

This shuts your Mac down. You can also shut down your Mac by pressing the Power-On button, which will open a dialog box with the options for restarting, shutting down, or putting your Mac to sleep.

Log Out

This option logs you out of your system, taking you back to a login screen. The keyboard shortcut to log out is Shift-⌘-Q.

TIP

Sleep, Restart, Shutdown, and Log Out have moved from Mac OS 9's Special menu into Mac OS X's Apple menu. If you're looking for a menu option for Empty Trash, you will need to be in the Finder (Finder → Empty Trash, or Shift-⌘-Delete).

Think System Preferences, Not Control Panels

One of the most notable changes in Mac OS X is that the Control Panels (⌘ → Control Panels) aren't in the Apple menu. The Control Panels of old are now replaced by System Preferences. Table 1 lists the Control Panels from Mac OS 9 and shows you their equivalents in Mac OS X.

Table 1. Mac OS 9's Control Panels and their disposition in Mac OS X

Mac OS 9 Control Panel	Equivalent in Mac OS X
Appearance	System Preferences → Desktop System Preferences → General
Apple Menu Options	System Preferences → General
AppleTalk	System Preferences → Network → AppleTalk
ColorSync	System Preferences → ColorSync
Control Strip	Gone; think Dock
Date & Time	System Preferences → Date & Time
DialAssist[a]	System Preferences → Network → Show → Internal Modem
Energy Saver[a]	System Preferences → Energy Saver
Extensions Manager	Gone. With Mac OS X, you no longer need to manage your extensions. To view the extensions on your system, launch the Apple System Profiler (*/Applications/Utilities*), and click on the Extensions tab.
File Exchange	Gone
File Sharing	System Preferences → Sharing
File Synchronization	Gone
General Controls	System Preferences → General
Infrared	System Preferences → Network → Show → infrared-port
Internet	System Preferences → Internet
Keyboard	System Preferences → Keyboard System Preferences → International → Keyboard Menu
Keychain Access	Applications → Utilities → Keychain Access
Launcher	Gone; think Dock
Location Manager[a]	System Preferences → Network → Location (This only applies to network settings, unlike Location Manager.) → Location
Memory[a]	Gone
Modem[a]	System Preferences → Network → Show → Internal Modem
Monitors	System Preferences → Displays

Table 1. Mac OS 9's Control Panels and their disposition
in Mac OS X (continued)

Mac OS 9 Control Panel	Equivalent in Mac OS X
Mouse	System Preferences → Mouse
Multiple Users[a]	System Preferences → Users System Preferences → Login → Login Window
Numbers	System Preferences → International → Numbers
Password Security[a]	Available on new machines via open firmware
QuickTime Settings	System Preferences → QuickTime
Remote Access[a]	Applications → Internet Connect
Software Update	System Preferences → Software Update
Sound	System Preferences → Sound
Speech	System Preferences → Speech
Startup Disk	System Preferences → Startup Disk
TCP/IP	System Preferences → Network
Text	System Preferences → International → Language
Trackpad[a]	System Preferences → Mouse → Trackpad

[a] Not available under Classic.

See the "System Preferences" section, later in this book, for additional information about each control.

Other Missing Items

Some other things you'll find missing from Mac OS X include:

Apple CD Audio Player
> This has been replaced by iTunes.

The Chooser
> To configure a printer in Mac OS X, you will need to use the Print Center (*/Applications/Utilities*). To connect to a server or another computer on your network, you will need to use Go → Connect to Server (⌘-K). The Chooser still exists for printing and networking from the Classic environment (described later).

Put Away (⌘-Y)

This command had two functions: to eject a disk (floppy or CD), or to move an item out of the Trash back to its place of origin. Instead, ⌘-E can be used to eject a CD or unmount a networked drive.

TIP

On some newer hardware, F12 can be used to eject a CD or DVD.

Graphing Calculator

Gone; no replacement.

Note Pad and SimpleText

These have been replaced by the much more versatile TextEdit application.

Scrapbook

The Scrapbook has gone to the scrap heap.

SimpleSound

This has been replaced by the Sound panel, which can be accessed from System Preferences → Sound → Alerts.

Tips for Windows and Unix Converts

This section is intended as a quick reference guide for people who are coming to Mac OS X from a non-Mac platform (i.e., Windows and other Unix systems). We've tried to point out some key differences between your old platform and Mac OS X to help you acclimate yourself with the Mac that now sits before you.

- The Mac user interface has only one menu bar—at the top of the screen—instead of one on each window. The menu bar's contents change depending on which application is currently active. The name of the application that's currently active appears in bold text next to the Apple menu.

- The Apple menu, located at the far left of the menu bar, is roughly analogous to the Windows Start menu (although it doesn't list common utility programs).

- The basic GUI control program, akin to the Windows Explorer or the Window Manager in Windows, is called the Finder. Clicking on its icon in the Dock (the blue smiley-face icon) brings up a Finder window, not the desktop as you might expect.

- To find what Mac OS X applications you have on your system, click on the Applications icon in the Finder's toolbar.

- To find out which Mac OS 9 applications you have on your system, click on Finder → Computer → Mac OS 9.2.2 → Applications (Mac OS 9).

- The Command key (⌘) provides many of the functions that you are used to having associated with the Control key. For example, use ⌘-C to copy, not Control-C; ⌘-S to save, not Control-S, etc. In the Terminal application, however, the Control key will perform the expected functions.

- At first, you will sorely miss your two- or three-button mouse. You can emulate right-button functions by holding down the Control key when clicking, or you probably can still use your two-button mouse if it's USB. Mac OS X supports multibutton mice, mapping the Control key to the right mouse button.

- The Dock is analogous to the Windows Task Bar. It is initially populated with some frequently accessed applications, such as the Finder, System Preferences, and Sherlock (the Mac file search application). You can drag any program icon onto the Dock to create a shortcut to it accessible at all times.

- System Preferences is analogous to the Windows Control Panel. The System Preferences application can be launched by clicking on its icon in the Dock (the one that looks like a light switch with a gray apple next to it).

- Printer setup and queue control is handled by the Print Center application (*/Applications/Utilities*). You may want to drag it onto the Dock or place its icon in the Finder toolbar for easy access.

- Each user has his own desktop, which is stored in */Users/ username/Desktop*. By default, many documents (such as files downloaded from the Web or saved attachments) are stored in */Users/username/Documents*. Files stored in the Desktop folder will appear on the desktop when you log in.

- The Unix command line (the *tcsh* shell) is available via the Terminal application (*/Applications/Utilities*). If you plan to work frequently from the command line, you should add the Terminal application's icon to the Dock by dragging its icon there.

- For Unix users and administrators, you'll quickly find out that some of your admin commands are missing or that useful options aren't there. For example, the commands for managing users and groups don't exist; for that, you need to use the GUI tools and/or NetInfo Manager (*/Applications/Utilities*).

- To find out which Unix applications and utilities are available, you can poke around in */usr/bin*, */usr/local/bin*, */usr/sbin*, */usr/share*, and */usr/libexec*.

- By default, the *root* user (or *superuser*) isn't activated. If you are the only user on your system, chances are you will have administrator privileges for using the *sudo* command. See "The root User Account" later in this book for details on how to activate the *root* user.

- While Mac OS X is Unix-based, it doesn't come with the X Window System. Don't fret, though. You can download and install a rootless version of X, but first you should download and install Fink (*http://fink.sourceforge.net*), which you can use to download and automatically install BSD Unix applications.

PART II

Mac OS X Basics

This part of the book will introduce you to the key features of the Mac OS X interface. Here we'll cover:

- Window Controls
- The Finder
- Keyboard shortcuts
- The Dock
- Mac OS X and the Classic Environment
- Users and Logging in Window Controls

Window Controls

Windows in Mac OS X have an entirely different set of controls than those from earlier versions of the Mac OS. These window features are highlighted in Figure 2.

The controls are defined as follows:

1. Close window button
2. Minimize window button
3. Zoom, or maximize, window button
4. Proxy icon
5. Filename
6. Scrollbars and scroll arrows
7. Window resize control

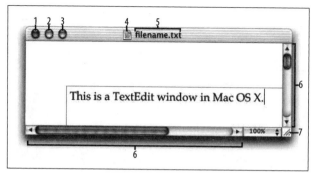

Figure 2. Standard window controls in Mac OS X

Window Tips

The following are some tips for working with windows:

Open a new window?
    File → Open (⌘-O)

Close a window?
    File → Close (⌘-W)

Close all open windows for an application?
    Option-click on the close window button.

TIP

If there are changes that need to be saved in any of the windows being closed, you will be prompted to save the changes. Either hit Return to save the changes, or enter ⌘-D to invoke the Don't Save button.

Minimize a window?
    Window → Minimize Window (⌘-M)

    Double-click on the window's titlebar.

Minimize all open windows for a single application?
    Option-⌘-M

NOTE

Issuing Option-⌘-M in Microsoft Word (Office v.X)
will open the Paragraph format window (Format →
Paragraph).

*Quickly create an alias of an open file, or move it, depending
on the app (e.g., Word)?*

Click on the file's icon in the window's titlebar, and drag
the icon to a new location (i.e., the Desktop, Dock,
Finder, etc.). The file must first be saved and named
before an alias can be created.

The Finder

In earlier versions of the Mac OS, the Finder could be found
in the application menu, located at the far-right edge of the
menu bar. The Finder was the application responsible for
displaying the contents of a drive or folder; when double-
clicked, a window would open, displaying either an Icon or
List View of the contents. Functionally, Mac OS X's Finder
really isn't that different from Mac OS 9's Finder. It is still
responsible for displaying the contents of drives and folders;
however, the Finder is much more powerful.

The Finder serves as a graphical file manager, which offers
three ways (or *Views*) to look at the files, folders, and applications on your system. The Finder also sports a toolbar that
allows you quick access to frequently used files and directories. More on the Finder toolbar later; for now, let's look at
the three Views available to the Finder: Icon, List, and the
new Column View.

Icon View

This shows the contents of a directory as either a file,
folder, or application icon, as shown in Figure 3. Double-
clicking on an icon will do one of three things: launch an
application, open a file, or display the contents of a
double-clicked folder in the Finder window.

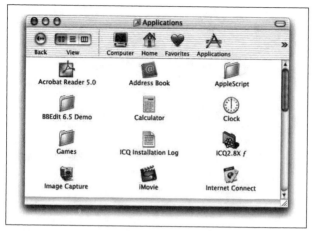

Figure 3. The Finder in Icon View

Table 2 presents a list of keyboard shortcuts that can be used within the Finder's Icon View.

Table 2. Icon View's keyboard shortcuts

Key command	Description
Up, Down, Left, and Right Arrow keys	Move through the icons in the view based on the key pressed.
Shift-Arrow key	When one icon is selected and the Shift-Arrow (Up, Down, Left, or Right) keys are pressed, the icon in that direction will be selected as well.

List View

A directory's contents are displayed in a list, as shown in Figure 4. To display the contents of a folder, you can click on the disclosure triangle (the black triangle to the left of the folder), as illustrated in the figure.

Another way to navigate through the icons and folders in the Finder's List View is by using the keyboard, as noted in Table 3.

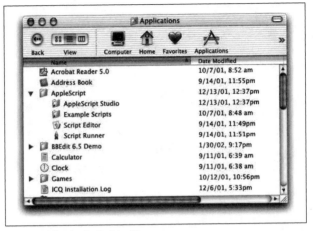

Figure 4. The Finder in List View

Table 3. List View's keyboard shortcuts

Key command	Description
Down Arrow	Move down through the list of items
Up Arrow	Move up through the list of items
Right Arrow	Open a folder's disclosure triangle to reveal its contents
Left Arrow	Close a folder's disclosure triangle to hide its contents
Option-Right Arrow	Open a folder and any subfolders
Option-Left Arrow	Close a folder and any subfolders

To open all of the folders in the View, select all of the View's contents (⌘-A), and use Option-Right arrow (likewise, use Option-Left arrow to close them again).

Column View

For NeXT users, the Column View will look familiar. Column View, shown in Figure 5, displays a directory's contents in column form. This is similar to List View, except that when you click on an item, a new pane opens to the right and either exposes the contents of a folder or displays some information about a file, including its name, type, and file size.

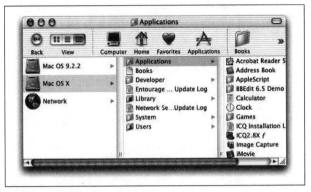

Figure 5. The Finder in Column View

Table 4 lists the keyboard shortcuts that can be used within the Finder's Column View.

Table 4. Column View's keyboard shortcuts

Key command	Description
Up, Down, Left, Right Arrow keys	Move through the columns in the View based on the key pressed

The Finder Toolbar

Near the top of the Finder window is a toolbar (shown in Figure 6), which offers a quick way to access files and directories on your system and also to switch between the View modes mentioned earlier.

You can add a file, folder, or application to the Finder toolbar by dragging and dropping its icon to the toolbar. Application icons that get added to the toolbar will launch with a single click, just as they do in the Dock.

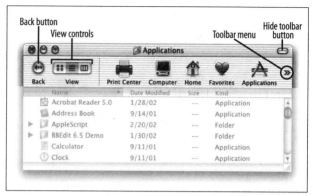

Figure 6. The Finder toolbar

Located at the upper-right corner of the Finder window is a clear, elliptical button that can be used to hide the Finder's toolbar, as shown in Figure 7.

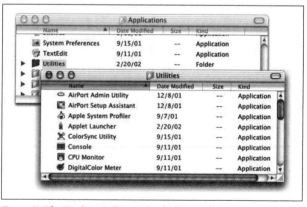

Figure 7. The Finder window with a hidden toolbar

With the toolbar hidden, the Finder window performs just like the Icon and List View windows in Mac OS 9. Double-clicking on a folder icon will open a new window for that folder, displaying its contents. Column View will function normally.

Finder Tips

The following are some tips for working with the Finder:

Hide the Finder toolbar?
    View → Hide Toolbar (⌘-B)

    Click on the transparent button in the upper-right corner of the titlebar.

Customize the Finder toolbar?
    Finder → View → Customize Toolbar

    Shift-click the Hide Toolbar button.

Add an icon for the Trash to the Finder's toolbar?
    Click on the Trash icon in the Dock to open a Finder window, and drag the Trash icon in the titlebar to the Finder toolbar.

I've decided I don't want the Trash icon in my Finder toolbar, but I can't drag it away. Help!
    ⌘-drag the Trash icon away from the toolbar to make it disappear.

Only show the icons or text labels of items in the toolbar?
    View → Customize Toolbar → Show; select Icons Only or Text Only from the pull-down menu.

Locate a specific folder in the Finder?
    Go → Go to Folder (or ⌘-~)

Keyboard Shortcuts

On the Mac (as with Windows and Linux desktops), you have two ways of invoking commands in the GUI: by using the menus or by issuing shortcuts for the commands on the keyboard. Not every menu item has a keyboard accelerator, but for the ones that do—the more commonly used functions—using the keyboard shortcuts can save you a lot of time.

Basic Keyboard Shortcuts

Table 5 lists the common key commands found in Mac OS X. While most of these commands work across all applications, some, like ⌘-B and ⌘-I, can be different from program to program, and others may only work when the Finder is active. For example, ⌘-B in Microsoft Word will turn on boldface type or make a selection bold, while in Project Builder, ⌘-B will build your application. Likewise, ⌘-I in Word will italicize a word or selection, while hitting ⌘-I after selecting a file, folder, or application on the Desktop or in the Finder will open the Show Info window for the selected item.

Table 5. Common keyboard shortcuts

Task	Key command
Open the Force Quit window	Option-⌘-Escape
Cycle through active applications in the Dock	⌘-Tab
Cancel operation	⌘-.
Open Mac Help	⌘-?
Go back in the Finder view to the previous item	⌘-[
Go to folder	⌘-~
Select all	⌘-A
Hide Finder's toolbar	⌘-B
Copy	⌘-C
Duplicate; creates a duplicate copy of a selected item. This command will add the word "copy" to the filename before the file extension. For example, if you were to select the file *file.txt* and hit ⌘-D, a new file named *file copy.txt* (with a space in the filename) would be created in the same directory as *file.txt*.	⌘-D
Turn Dock hiding on/off	Option-⌘-D
Move item to Trash	⌘-Delete
Empty Trash	Shift-Option-Delete
Eject the selected disk image, CD, etc.	⌘-E
Find	⌘-F
Hide application	⌘-H

Table 5. Common keyboard shortcuts (continued)

Task	Key command
Show Info	⌘-I
Show View options in the Finder. (Note: there are no options for the Column View; what you see is what you get.)	⌘-J
Connect to Server	⌘-K
Make alias	⌘-L
Minimize window	⌘-M
Minimize all open windows for an application	Option-⌘-M
Open a new Finder window. (This is a change from earlier versions of the Mac OS where ⌘-N was used to create new folders.)	⌘-N
Create new folder	Shift-⌘-N
Open file or folder; can also be used to launch applications.	⌘-O
Print file	⌘-P
Quit application	⌘-Q
Show original	⌘-R
Add to Favorites	⌘-T
Paste	⌘-V
Close window	⌘-W
Close all windows	Option-⌘-W
Cut	⌘-X
Undo	⌘-Z
Redo (not available in all applications)	Shift-⌘-Z
Go to Applications view in the Finder	Option-⌘-A
Go to Computer view in the Finder	Option-⌘-C
Go to Favorites view in the Finder	Option-⌘-F
Go to Home view in the Finder	Option-⌘-H
Go to iDisk view in the Finder	Option-⌘-I
Take a screenshot of the entire display	Shift-⌘-3
Make and capture a rectangular selection of the display	Shift-⌘-4

The Dock

One way to think about the Dock is as part Finder, part Apple menu, and part Launcher from earlier versions of the Mac OS. The Dock, shown in Figure 8, holds application aliases, making it easy for you to launch a program quickly with a single mouse click. To launch an application in the Dock, simply click on its icon. While the application is starting, its icon will "bounce" in the Dock; afterward, a black triangle will appear below the icon to indicate that the application is active.

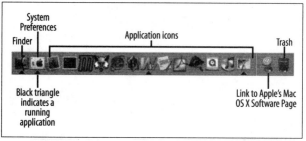

Figure 8. The Dock

To add an application icon to the Dock, simply drag its icon from the Finder to any location in the Dock and let go. To remove an application, click on the icon and drag it away from the Dock; the icon will disappear in a puff of smoke.

The Dock is also home to the Finder, System Preferences, Sherlock, and the Trash.

NOTE

The Finder icon is permanently fixed to the left of the Dock (or on top if you've moved your Dock to the left or right of the screen). Likewise, the Trash is located at the far-right of the Dock (or at the bottom if your Dock is on the left or right). No matter how hard you try to grab and move them around, you can't. Also, you can't place an icon to the left of the Finder or to the right of the Trash.

Using and Configuring the Dock

Here are some helpful hints and tips for using and configuring your Dock:

Change the Dock's preferences?
    → Dock → Dock Preferences

    System Preferences → Dock

Add a program to the Dock?
    Drag and drop an application's icon in the Dock.

    After launching an application that isn't normally in the Dock, Control-click on an application's icon, and select "Keep in Dock" from the pop-up menu.

Remove a program from the Dock?
    Drag the application icon from the Dock, and drop it anywhere.

Change the Dock's location from the bottom of the screen to the left or right side?
    System Preferences → Dock → Position on screen

    → Dock → Position on Left (or Position on Right)

Control the magnification of icons in the Dock?
    System Preferences → Dock → Magnification

    → Dock → Turn Magnification (On/Off)

Make it so the Dock hides when I'm not using it?
    System Preferences → Dock → Automatically hide and show the Dock

    → Dock → Turn Hiding On

    Option-⌘-D

Stop application icons from bouncing when a program is launched?
    System Preferences → Dock → Animate opening applications. Instead of the application's icon bouncing, the disclosure triangle next to the icon will pulse until the program is fully launched.

Dock Tricks

The following key-mouse commands can be used when clicking on an icon in the Dock:

Command-click

> If you ⌘-click an application icon in the Dock (or just click and hold down the mouse button), the Finder will open, taking you to that application's folder.

Control-click

> If you Control-click a running application in the Dock (or click and hold down the mouse button), a pop-up menu will open, listing the windows that the application has open, as well as options to show the application in the Finder and to Quit the application.

> If you press the Option key while Control-clicking an icon in the Dock, the Quit option will toggle to Force Quit. This will not work for Classic applications (i.e., it only works for native Mac OS X applications).

Option-click

> Option-clicking has the same effect as Control-clicking, with one exception: Quit has been replaced by Force Quit in the pop-up menu.

Command-Tab

> The ⌘-Tab function allows you to cycle through and switch between running applications quickly. As you press ⌘-Tab, the icons for running applications will highlight; when you release the ⌘ key, you will be taken to that application.

Shift-⌘-Tab

> Shift-⌘-Tab has the reverse effect of ⌘-Tab, in that it moves backward through running applications in the Dock.

Mac OS X and the Classic Environment

To help bridge the application gap between Mac OS 9 and Mac OS X, Apple has built a *virtual machine* that enables you to run older Mac software under Mac OS X in what's known as *Classic*. Classic (or the "Classic environment") looks and feels just like Mac OS 9. The only exception is that the applications that are run in Classic don't benefit from the features of Mac OS X, such as protected memory and its advanced printing capability. Additionally, some Control Panels (⬧ → Control Panels), such as Control Strip, Memory, and Remote Access, are disabled.* Basically, when you're running Classic, you are running a slightly watered-down version of Mac OS 9 *on top of* Mac OS X with only a minor performance hit.

Until all Mac applications are compliant with Mac OS X, you will also need to install a version of Mac OS 9 (9.2.2, to be exact). During the installation process, you can either create a separate partition (or have a separate hard drive) for Mac OS 9 *and* Mac OS X, or you can install both operating systems on the same partition. Basically, you're creating a *dual-boot system*, which means you can boot your Mac into either OS. However, if you don't plan to run Classic applications, you won't need to install Mac OS 9.

If your computer came with Mac OS X preinstalled, Mac OS 9 will be preinstalled as well. It's worth noting that Apple places both Mac OS X and Mac OS 9 on the same partition of your

---

* However, if you boot into Mac OS 9 instead of Mac OS X, you will be using a full version of the OS. See later for details on how to choose your Startup Disk.

hard drive. If you want the OSes on separate partitions, you will need to partition your hard drive and reinstall the system. In most cases, the biggest benefit of installing Mac OS 9 and Mac OS X on separate partitions is being able to choose a startup volume at boot up by holding down the Option key. Otherwise, you can choose which OS to boot using the Startup Disk Control Panel (Mac OS 9) or System Preferences → Startup Disk (Mac OS X).

NOTE

If you use the ProcessViewer or the *top* command, described later, look for a process named *TruBlue-Environment*. This is the Classic process—and all the applications running under Classic—in action.

To launch a Classic application, locate the application using the Finder (Finder → Mac OS 9.2.2 → Applications (Mac OS 9)), and double-click on the application icon. The Classic environment will start if it isn't already running.

TIP

If you frequently use a particular Classic application, you can also add it to the Dock by dragging its icon to any location in the Dock.

While it's easy to use a Classic application on files saved on your Mac OS X partition, you will have a hard time accessing files saved on non-AFP networked drives. For example, if you're running Office 2001 and you want to open a Word document (*filename.doc*) on the drive *Maui*, you won't find that drive in Word 2001's Open dialog. So, what can you do? Fortunately, you can use the Terminal application to launch Word 2001 *and* open the file in one fell swoop. To do this, launch the Terminal application (*/Applications/Utilities*), and issue the following command on the command line:

```
open /Volumes/Maui/filename.doc
```

This command instructs your computer to open *filename.doc* (found on */Volumes/Maui*) using Microsoft Word. For more information about how to use the Terminal application, see "Configuring and Using the Terminal" later in this book.

Users and Logging In

The ability to have multiple users on the same system was first introduced with Mac OS 9, but it wasn't mandatory as it is with Mac OS X.

Tips for Users

Here are some helpful hints to assist you in managing your user account:

Configuring my login?
System Preferences → Login

Change my login password?
System Preferences → Users → *username* → Edit User → Password panel

Use the *passwd* command in the Terminal.

NOTE

When choosing a password, you should avoid using dictionary words (i.e., common, everyday words found in the dictionary) or something that could be easily guessed. To improve your security, we recommend that you choose an alpha-numeric password. Remember, passwords are case-sensitive, so you can mix upper- and lowercase letters with your password as well.

Add another user to the system?
System Preferences → Users → New User (requires administrator privileges)

Remove a user from the system?

System Preferences → Users → *username* → Delete User (requires administrator privileges). After a user has been deleted, that user's directories (and everything within) becomes the property of the *root* user; only *root* can delete these directories from the system.

I've deleted a user, but that person's directories still exist and I can't move them to Trash in the Finder. How can I delete them?

When you delete a user, that user's directories become the property of the *root* user, and you'll see something like *max Deleted* in the Users directory in the Finder (where *max* is the name of the user whose account was deleted). To delete these directories, you will need to use the Terminal and log in as *root*, then remove the directories as follows:

```
[localhost:/Users] chuck% ls
Shared     chuck     max Deleted
[lcoalhost:/Users] chuck% su
Password: ********
[localhost:/Users] root# rm -r max\ Deleted/
[localhost:/Users] root# ls
Shared     chuck
```

```
[localhost:/Users] root# exit
exit
[localhost:/Users] chuck%
```

Give a user administrator privileges?

System Preferences → Users → *username* → Password panel → Allow user to administer this computer (requires administrator privileges)

Turn off automatic login?

System Preferences → Login → Login Window; uncheck the box next to "Automatically log in"

Set a password hint?

System Preferences → Users → *username* → Edit User → Password → Password Hint

Find out which users have admin privileges?

Applications → Utilities → NetInfo Manager

In the Directory Browser pane, select / → groups → admin, then look in the Directory /admin pane below, and look at the property value next to users. (Requires administrator privileges.)

Add a new group?

Applications → Utilities → NetInfo Manager

In the Directory Browser pane, select / → groups, then go to Directory → New Subdirectory (⌘-N). (Requires administrator privileges.)

In the Directory pane below, select the *new_directory* name by double-clicking on it, type in a new group name (e.g., *editorial*), and then click again on *new_directory* in the Directory Browser pane. A warning message will appear, asking you if you want to save the changes (click Save). Another message window will appear, asking you to Confirm the Modification; click on Update this copy, and the new group name will be applied in the Directory Browser pane.

User Subdirectories

Once created, each user is provided with a series of subdirectories in his *Home* directory (*/Users/username*). These directories, listed here, can be used for storing anything your heart desires, although some have specific purposes.

Desktop
> This directory contains the items found on your Desktop, including any files, folders, or application aliases you've placed there.

Documents
> While it isn't mandatory, the *Documents* directory can be used as a repository for any files or folders you create.

Library
> This directory is similar to the */System/Preferences* directory found in earlier versions of the Mac OS; it contains resources used by applications, but not the applications themselves.

Public
> If you enable file or web sharing (System Preferences → Sharing), this is where you can place items you wish to share with other users. Users who access your *Public* directory can see and copy items from this directory.

Movies
> This is a place where you can store movies you create with iMovie or hold QuickTime movies you create or download from the Internet.

Music

> This directory can be used to store music and sound files, including *.aiff*, *.mp3*, etc. This is also where the iTunes Library is located.

Pictures

> This directory can be used as a place to store photos and other images. iPhoto also uses the Pictures directory to house its iPhoto Library directory, which contains the photo albums you create. This is also a good place to store pictures for any screensavers you create.

Sites

> If you enable Web Sharing (System Preferences → Sharing → File & Web), this is the directory that will house the web site for your user account.

The root User Account

On any Unix system, the *root* user has the authority to issue any command, giving that user extreme power. Because of that, and the risks associated with that power (such as the ability to delete the entire filesystem permanently), the *root* user account has been disabled by default on Mac OS X. However, there are two ways you can enable the *root* user account: by using NetInfo Manager or from the command line. In both cases, you must already have administrator privileges on the system.*

Follow these steps to enable the *root* user account from NetInfo Manager:

1. Launch NetInfo Manager (*/Applications/Utilities*).

2. To make changes to the NetInfo settings, click on the padlock in the lower-left corner of the NetInfo window. You will be asked for the administrator's name and password; enter those, and click OK.

---

* If you're the only user on the system, you should have administrator privileges by default.

3. In the menu bar, select Domain → Security → Enable Root User.

4. You will be asked to enter a password for the *root* user. Unlike user passwords, the password for the *root* user must be eight characters or less. Click OK, and then enter the password again to confirm the password for the *root* user account. Click on the Verify button to confirm the password and enable the *root* account.

5. If you have no further changes to make in NetInfo Manager, click on the padlock at the lower-left of the window, and quit the application (⌘-Q).

To enable the *root* user account using the Terminal, enter the following command:

```
[localhost:~] chuck% sudo passwd root
Password: *******
Changing password for root.
New password: ********
Retype new password: ********
[localhost:~] chuck%
```

The first time you're asked for a password, enter your own. Once you're verified by the system to have administrator privileges, you will be asked to enter and confirm a new password for the *root* user account.

NOTE

The asterisks shown in this example won't appear on-screen when you enter the passwords; actually, nothing will happen onscreen. If you make a mistake while entering the password, you can always hit the Backspace or Delete key to go back over what you typed; then just re-enter the password.

Once the *root* account has been assigned a password, you can use it to log in with the username *root*.

If you find that you need to access a directory or issue a command that requires root (or *superuser*) privileges, you can temporarily log in as the *root* user using the *su* command:

```
[localhost:~] chuck% su
Password: ********
[localhost:/Users/chuck] root#
```

Notice how the prompt has changed from chuck% to root#. After you've finished doing your business as *root*, type *exit*, and hit Return to log out as the *root* user and return to your normal user prompt.

NOTE

The *root* user's home directory can be found in */private/var/root*.

Show Info and Setting File Permissions

Show Info gives you access to all sorts of information about the files, directories, and applications on your system. To view the information for an item, click on its icon in the Finder, and either go to File → Show Info or use its keyboard shortcut, ⌘-I. The Show Info window has a pull-down menu, which offers the following options:

General Information
> This tells you the basics about the file, including its file type, where it's located, how big it is, and when it was created and last modified.

Name & Extension
> This displays a text box with the name of the file or directory.

Open with Application
> This option is only available if you select a file (i.e., not a folder or an application). Here you can specify which application will open this file or all similar files.

Preview

Depending on the file type, you can view the contents of the file here (this also works for playing sounds and QuickTime movies).

Privileges

This will display the name of the owner and the name of the group to which the file belongs. It will also allow you to set access privileges to that file for the Owner, Group, and Everyone on the system.

The Show Info pull-down menu for applications will have the General Information, Name & Extension, and Privileges options mentioned previously (although the Privileges options will be disabled), as well as one or both of the following options:

Languages

Shows the languages supported by that application.

Plugins

Lists the available plug-ins for the application.

Noticeably missing from a Mac OS X application's Show Info window is the Memory option. Since memory for applications is assigned dynamically by virtual memory, you no longer have to specify (in the Get Info box) how much memory an application will require. However, if you use Show Info on a Mac OS 9 application, the Memory option will be there.

PART III

System Tools

This part of the book introduces you to the various tools that accompany Mac OS X. The sections in this part are intended to provide an overview of the following:

- System Preferences
- Applications and Utilities
- Developer Tools

Part V provides additional information about how to use and apply the System Preferences for configuring your system, as well as specific uses for some of Mac OS X's standard Applications and Utilities.

System Preferences

As mentioned earlier, Mac OS X's System Preferences perform many of the same functions as Mac OS 9's Control Panels. To launch the System Preferences application, simply click on the light-switch icon in the Dock, and the window shown in Figure 9 will appear.

As you'll notice, the System Preferences are broken down into four categories: Personal, Hardware, Internet & Network, and System. There is also a customizable toolbar at the top of the window, similar to the toolbar in the Finder window. If you find yourself using a particular System Preference often, drag its icon to the toolbar. Likewise, if there is one you use rarely (such as the Displays panel), drag the icon away, and the item will be removed from the toolbar.

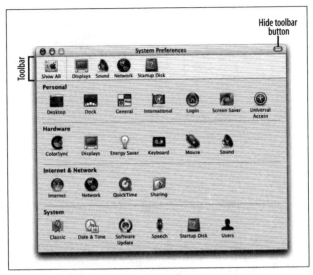

Figure 9. The System Preferences window

When you click on one of the icons, the window will change to reflect that particular item's settings, but the toolbar will remain in place. To hide the toolbar, click on the transparent button in the upper-right corner of the window. To go back to the main view, click the Show All button (or use View → Show All, or ⌘-L). When you've completed altering the settings of your computer, quit the System Preferences (System Prefs → Quit, or ⌘-Q).

The next four sections provide an overview of the controls found in the System Preferences.

For additional information on how to use the System Preferences panels to configure your system, see the "Task and Setting Index" later in the book.

NOTE

Some of the System Preferences panels require administrator privileges. If you attempt to change a setting and are asked for a password, try using the password you used to log in to the computer. If that doesn't work, you will need to contact your system administrator for assistance.

Personal

These items are used to control the general look and feel of the Aqua interface:

Desktop
This lets you set the pattern, image, or color of your desktop.

Dock
This is one of the ways you can configure your Dock (another is by going to → Dock → Dock Preferences). See the section, "Using and Configuring the Dock," earlier in the book, for details on the Dock.

General
This panel specifies the colors used for buttons and menu items when selected, location of scrollbar arrows (top and bottom, or together, known as "Smart Scrolling" in Mac OS 9), and how a click in the scrollbar will be interpreted (scroll down one page or scroll to that location in the document). Here, you can specify the number of recent items to be remembered and listed in the → Recent Items menu for Applications and Documents, as well as determine at which font size anti-aliasing will be turned off.

International

Used to set non-English (U.S.) language support. Also found here are controls used to format the date, time, numbers, and currency, as well as the keyboard layout to be used for a country and its language.

Login

This panel allows you to configure your login settings, described earlier.

Screen Saver

This panel can be used to select one of Mac OS X's default screensaver modules. Here, you can set the amount of time your system must be inactive before the screensaver kicks in, require a password to turn off the screensaver, and specify Hot Corners for enabling/disabling the screensaver.

Universal Access

The Universal Access panel provides support for people who have a physical disability that makes it difficult to use a keyboard or mouse. Here, you can turn on Sticky Keys, making possible to issue keyboard shortcuts one keystroke at a time or use the numeric keypad instead of a mouse.

Hardware

These panels are used to control the settings for the devices connected to your computer.

ColorSync

This panel is used to control and ensure the quality of the colors you see on your monitor.

Displays

The Displays panel lets you set your monitor's resolution (640 × 480, 800 × 600, or 1024 × 768) and its color-depth (256, thousands, or millions of colors). There is also an option to include a monitor menulet in the menu bar, as well as a slider control to set your monitor's brightness.

Energy Saver

This panel is used to set the auto-sleep settings for you computer. Here, you can specify the amount of time your system must be idle before putting your monitor, hard drive, or the entire system to sleep.

Keyboard Access

This panel controls the repeat rate when you depress a key and hold it down. You can specify the speed of the repeat (from slow to fast) and the delay between the time the key is first depressed until the repeat option kicks in (from long to short). If you select the Off option for Delay Until Repeat, the repeat feature will be disabled entirely.

If you click on the Full Keyboard Access tab and opt to "Turn on full keyboard access," you can use the Control key with either Function keys or Letter keys instead of using the mouse. These key combinations and their functions are listed in Table 6.

Table 6. Keyboard Access key combinations

Combination	Description
Control-F1	Enable/disable Keyboard Access
Control-F2	Control the menu bar
Control-F3	Control the Dock
Control-F4	Activate the window or the next window behind it
Control-F5	Control an application's toolbar
Control-F6	Control an application's utility window (or palette)
Control-F7	Used for windows and dialogs to highlight either text input fields and lists, or for any window control
Esc	Return control to the mouse, disabling the Control-F*x* key combination
Spacebar	Perform the function of a mouse click

Mouse

This panel lets you specify settings for using your Mouse and/or Trackpad (if you're using a laptop). Both tabs allow you to specify the speed of the mouse, as well as set the delay between double-clicks.

Sound

The Sound panel offers two panes, one for configuring Alert sounds and another for sound Output (e.g., speakers). The Alerts pane has an option for including a volume control slider in the menu bar.

Internet & Network

These panels are used to control your Mac's settings for connecting to other computers:

Internet

The Internet panel has four tabs that allow you to configure the settings for your iTools account (or to set one up if you haven't already), Email, Web, and News. This is where you enter the settings for your email account, specify your default email and news client or web browser, and where files downloaded from the Internet will be saved.

Network

This panel is used to configure your settings for dial-up, Ethernet, and AirPort networking, including enabling/disabling AppleTalk. For details on how to configure these settings, see the "Task and Setting Index" later in this book.

QuickTime

This panel lets you configure QuickTime's settings for playing back movies and music. If you've purchased a license for QuickTime Pro, click on the Registration button to enter the registration number.

Sharing

This panel allows file, application, and web sharing.

System

The items in the System panel allow you to configure a variety of settings for your computer:

Classic

Use this to start, stop, and restart the Classic environment. For additional information, see "Mac OS X and the Classic Environment," earlier in this book.

Date & Time

This panel is used to set, obviously, the date and time for your system.

Software Update

As with Mac OS 9, the Software Update panel can be used to check for updates to your Mac OS X system. You can use this panel to check for updates manually (i.e., when you want to, or when you know of an available update) or automatically (daily, weekly, or monthly). When an update is found, you will be prompted to specify which updates will be downloaded and installed on your system.

Speech

This panel can be used to turn on speech recognition and to specify a default voice for applications that speak text.

Startup Disk

This panel is used to specify whether your system will boot into Mac OS 9 or Mac OS X.

Users

As the name implies, this panel is used to add and remove users and to make changes to their identity and password.

After you've completed tweaking your System Preferences, use ⌘-Q to Quit the application.

Applications and Utilities

Apple has included a set of native applications and utilities for Mac OS X. There are applications for such things as viewing and printing PDF files, basic word processing, sending and receiving email, and creating movies, as well as utilities to help you manage your system.

Use the Finder to locate the Applications (Finder → Mac OS X → Applications) and Utilities (Finder → Mac OS X → Applications → Utilities) on your system. You can quickly go to the Applications folder either by clicking on the Applications icon in the toolbar or by using the Option-⌘-A keyboard shortcut. Since there is no keyboard shortcut to the Utilities, you might consider dragging the Utilities folder icon to the Finder toolbar.

Applications

The following is a list of the programs found in the *Applications* directory:

Acrobat Reader
> This is Adobe Systems' application for viewing and printing PDF files.

Address Book
> The Address Book is a database program that you can use to store contact information for your friends and colleagues. By selecting a name in your address book, you can quickly send that person an email by clicking on the Send Mail button.

AppleScript
> This folder contains all of the tools necessary for writing AppleScripts. If you've downloaded or installed the Developer Tools (see later in this book), you will also have the ability to build applications using AppleScript Studio.

Calculator

This is a simple calculator, which performs basic math functions (add, subtract, multiply, and divide).

Chess

Based on GNU Chess, Apple has taken this Unix-based chess game and packaged it with a Cocoa interface and 3D game pieces.

Clock

Launching this application will place a Clock icon in the Dock. By changing the Clock's preferences, you can switch the display from analog to digital, display the time in 24-hour format (or military time), and set the clock to be a floating window on the desktop.

DVD Player

If your hardware natively supports DVD playback, the DVD Player will be installed. You can use this application to view DVD movies on your Mac.

Image Capture

This program can be used to download pictures from a digital camera to your Mac. It came with earlier versions of Mac OS X, but has since been replaced by the much more powerful (and versatile), iPhoto.

iMovie

iMovie is one of Apple's "iApplications" included with Mac OS X. Use iMovie to create digital movies on your Mac. To learn more about iMovie, see *iMovie 2: The Missing Manual* (Pogue Press/O'Reilly & Associates, 2001), or go to Apple's page at *http://www.apple.com/imovie*.

Internet Connect

This application is used for connecting to the Internet or to another computer via dial-up modem or an AirPort connection. It shows your current dial-up status and settings (as configured in the Network pane of your System Preferences) and provides a Connect/Disconnect button for opening or closing a connection.

Internet Explorer

Microsoft's Internet Explorer 5.1 acts as Mac OS X's default web browser.

iPhoto

iPhoto allows you to download, organize, and edit images taken with a digital camera. iPhoto is much more powerful than Image Capture, described earlier. To learn more about iPhoto, go to Apple's iPhoto page at *http:// www.apple.com/iphoto*.

iTunes

iTunes can be used to play CDs, to listen to Internet radio stations, to import (rip) music from CDs, to burn CDs from music you've collected, and to store and play MP3 files. If you have an iPod, you can also use iTunes to synchronize your MP3 music files. To learn more about iTunes, see Apple's page at *http://www.apple.com/itunes*.

Mail

This is the default email client for Mac OS X.

Preview

Preview is a simple image viewer that lets you open (and export) files that have been saved in a variety of image formats, including PICT, GIF, JPEG, and TIFF, to name a few. Preview can also be used for opening and viewing PDF files. You cannot print an image file from Preview.

QuickTime Player

This is used for playing QuickTime movies, as well as listening to QuickTime streaming audio and video.

Sherlock

Sherlock is a search program that can help you find files on your system or locate information on the Internet. If you index folders on your system (Find → Index Now), you can do content-based searches, which will look for specific keywords you provide *within* the indexed files.

Stickies

> Stickies is a simple application that lets you create sticky notes on your screen. Like the notes stuck to your desk or computer, Stickies can be used to store important notes and reminders.

System Preferences

> This is the System Preferences application, described earlier and throughout this book.

TextEdit

> TextEdit replaces the SimpleText application from earlier versions of the Mac OS and can serve as a real word processor capable of creating documents and saving them as plain (*.txt*) or rich (*.rtf*) text documents.

Utilities

The tools found in the Utilities folder can be used to help you manage your Mac:

AirPort Admin Utility

> This utility is used to administer AirPort Base Stations.

AirPort Setup Assistant

> This utility is used for configuring your system to connect to an AirPort wireless network.

Apple System Profiler

> The Apple System Profiler keeps track of the finer details about your system. Here, you can view information about your particular computer, the devices (e.g., Zip or Jaz drive, CD-ROM drives, etc.) and volumes (i.e., hard drives and partitions) connected to your Mac, as well as listings of the frameworks, extensions, and applications on your Mac.

Applet Launcher

> This utility lets you run Java applets on your Mac.

ColorSync Utility

This utility has three significant features. By pressing the Profile First Aid icon, it can be used to verify and repair your ColorSync settings. The Profiles icon keeps track of the ColorSync profiles for your system, and the Devices icon lets you see which ColorSync devices are connected, as well as the name and location of the current profile.

Console

The primary use of the Console application is to log the interactions between applications on your system and also with the operating system itself. If you enable crash logging (Console → Preferences → Crashes), the Console will open automatically when an application quits unexpectedly. The crash log created by the Console application can be used by developers to help debug their applications.

CPU Monitor

This is a simple meter that shows you the current load on your Mac's processor. If you have a dual-processor machine, there should be two meters.

DigitalColor Meter

The DigitalColor Meter is a small application that lets you view and copy the color settings for any pixel on your screen.

Directory Setup

This utility controls access for Mac OS X systems to directory services, such as NetInfo, LDAP, and Active Directory.

Disk Copy

This is a useful tool for creating disk images (*.dmg*) for batching up and sending files (including folders and applications) from one Mac user to another.

Disk Utility

This utility can be used to repair a damaged hard drive, as well as for initializing and partitioning new drives.

Display Calibrator

The Display Calibrator helps you calibrate your display to create a custom ColorSync profile.

Grab

The Grab utility can be used to take screenshots of your system. Two of its most useful features include the ability to select the pointer (or no pointer at all) to be displayed in the screenshot, as well as the ability to start a 10-second timer before the screenshot is taken to give you the necessary time to set up the shot.

Installer

This program launches whenever you install an application on your system.

Java Web Start

Java Web Start (or JWS) can be used to download and run Java applications.

Key Caps

Key Caps can be used to view the characters available for any font on your system. Different fonts contain different hidden characters; you can select a different font using the Fonts menu. See Table 20 in the section "Special Characters" for a listing of the keyboard shortcuts for creating special and international characters.

Keychain Access

This utility can be used to create and manage your passwords for accessing secure web and FTP sites, networked filesystems, and other items such as password-encoded files.

NetInfo Manager

The NetInfo Manager is mainly a tool for system and network administrators to view and edit the settings for a system. You need to have administrator privileges to use NetInfo Manager.

Network Utility

This utility is a graphical frontend to a standard set of Unix tools such as *netstat*, *ping*, *traceroute*, *whois*, and *finger*; it also lets you view specific information about your network connection and scan the available ports for a particular domain or IP address.

Print Center

The Print Center is the utility that configures and controls the printers connected to your computer. For users who are coming over from Mac OS 9, the Print Center replaces the Chooser for managing printers.

ProcessViewer

This program lets you view the processes running on your system. If you click on a process name, you can see additional information about that process by clicking on the disclosure triangle next to "More Info," or you can cancel (*kill*, in Unix-speak) by highlighting a process and choosing Processes → Quit Process (Shift-⌘-Q).

StuffIt Expander

StuffIt Expander is the popular utility for expanding, or decompressing, files. To launch StuffIt Expander, simply double-click on the compressed file.

Terminal

The Terminal application is the command-line interface (CLI) to Mac OS X's Unix core. For more information about the Terminal, see "Configuring and Using the Terminal" later in this book.

Developer Tools

Apple has gone to great lengths to lure a new breed of developers to the Mac, offering environments for traditional C, C++, Objective-C (and recently Objective-C++), Java, and with the introduction of AppleScript Studio, AppleScripters can now harness their scripting knowledge to build Cocoa-based applications.

Installing the Developer Tools

You can quickly check to see if you have the Developer Tools installed. If you have a */Developer* folder on your hard drive, you are ready to go. If not, you'll need to install the tools either from the Developer Tools CD that came with your system or from a disk image you can download from the Apple Developer Connection (ADC) site.

The Developer Tools CD comes with every boxed set of Mac OS X (including Mac OS X Server), as well as with new Macs shipped from the factory with OS X. To install the tools, simply find the CD (it's the gray one), put it into your CD-ROM drive, and double-click the *Developer.mpkg* file that will appear.

NOTE

If you didn't receive a Developer Tools CD with your new Mac, you may find *Developer.mpkg* in */Applications/Installers/Developer Tools*.

If you can't find your Developer Tools CD, or if you received a Mac OS X upgrade package that didn't include it (some of the free OS X 10.0 to 10.1 packages only came with one CD), you should go to the ADC member web site at *http://connect.apple.com* and download them.

ADC Membership has its privileges. There are many levels of membership available. The free Online membership gets you a good range of benefits, including access to the latest version of the Developer Tools and the ability to track bugs that you submit. You can register free of charge for Online membership at *http://connect.apple.com*.

To download the Tools, log in to the ADC Member web site, click on Download Software in the navigation bar, and then on the Mac OS X subcategory link that appears. From this page you can download the Developer Tools either in segments or in one big chunk. If you download the Tools in segments, simply double-click on the first segment, and StuffIt will launch and put all the segments together into one file.

The Tools are provided as a Disk Image (*.dmg*) file. When you double-click on a disk image, a temporary disk is mounted onto your system. Simply navigate to this disk in the Finder, and double-click on the *Developer.mpkg* file to launch the installer.

Overview of the Developer Tools

As noted in the previous section, the Developer Tools are installed in the */Developer/Applications* directory on your system. This section will briefly describe the more commonly used Tools:

Interface Builder
> Interface Builder is a GUI editor for both Cocoa and Carbon applications. It has complete online help and release notes, available by launching Project Builder and using the Help menu.

Project Builder
> Project Builder is an integrated development environment for Mac OS X. It supports both Cocoa and Carbon, using C, C++, Objective-C, and Java. It has complete online help and release notes, available by launching Project Builder and using the Help menu.

Project Builder for WebObjects
> Project Builder for WebObjects (or ProjectBuilderWO) should be used only by Web Objects developers.

FileMerge

FileMerge compares two files or directories and lets you merge them together.

PackageManager

PackageManager lets you package your software so that the Mac OS X Installer can install it on a user's machine.

IconComposer

IconComposer is used to create icon files (*.icns*) from existing images.

icns Browser

The icns Browser is used to display the contents of an *.icns* file.

PEFViewer

PEFViewer displays the contents of a PEF binary as a hexadecimal dump.

Pixie

Pixie displays a magnified image of whatever is under the mouse.

PropertyListEditor

PropertyListEditor lets you edit and create XML property lists.

For additional information about other development tools, including command-line and Java tools, see */Developer/ Documentation/DeveloperTools/DevToolsOverview.html*.

PART IV

Mac OS X Unix Basics

This part of the book serves as a basic introduction to show new users how to use the Unix side of Mac OS X. Specifically, this section will cover:

- Configuring and using the Terminal
- Command-line editing with *tcsh*
- Additional shell commands, like *bindkey*, *defaults*, and *open*
- Basic Unix commands

Configuring and Using the Terminal

The Terminal application (*/Applications/Utilities*) is your interface to Mac OS X's Unix shell. The Terminal can be used for everything from creating new directories (folders) and files to launching applications, and from managing and monitoring your system to programming and altering your system preferences.

Terminal Settings

This section offers advice on how to configure the settings for your Terminal:

Change the style of the cursor?
Terminal → Preferences → Text & Colors → Cursor Shape → (Block, Underline, Vertical Bar)

Stop the cursor from blinking?
Terminal → Preferences → Text & Colors → Options → Deselect Blinking Cursor

Change the background color and font colors of the Terminal window?
Terminal → Preferences → Text & Colors

Assign a different title to the Terminal window?
Terminal → Preferences → Window → Custom Title

Assign a different title to the current Terminal window?
With an open Terminal window, hit Shift-⌘-T (or Shell → Set Title). Select the Custom Title checkbox, and enter a new title in the text field.

Specify the number of lines a Terminal window can contain in the scrollback buffer?
Terminal → Preferences → Buffer → Scrollback Buffer

Set the Terminal's emulation mode to VT100?
Terminal → Preferences → Emulation → Strict VT100 emulation

NOTE

The interface says the VT100 mode isn't recommended, but it doesn't say why.

Close the Terminal window after I've exited?
Terminal → Preferences → Shell → Close the window if the shell exited cleanly

Change the shell from its default (tcsh)?
Terminal → Preferences → Shell → Use this shell; change */bin/tcsh* to either */bin/csh*, */bin/sh*, or */bin/zsh*

Where is the history file for the shell?
It's located in your home directory as *.tcsh_history*.

Where is the shell's configuration file located?
/usr/share/init/tcsh/rc

Can I create a customized shell environment that's different from the one used by other users on the system?

Yes, but read and follow the instructions in the *README* file located in */usr/share/init/tcsh*.

Keyboard Shortcuts

Table 7 lists the keyboard shortcuts that can be used with the Terminal application.

Table 7. Keyboard shortcuts for use with the Terminal

Key command	Description
⌘-. (period)	Terminate process (same as Control-C, the Unix interrupt command)
⌘-A	Select all of the text in the Terminal window
⌘-Up arrow	Scrolls up one line at a time
⌘-Down arrow	Scroll down one line at a time
⌘-I	Open the Terminal Inspector, which allows you to change some of the Terminal's settings
⌘-K	Clear all of the information from the Terminal window, disabling scrollback (this is different and more extensive than the *clear* command, described later)
⌘-Left arrow	Go to previous Terminal window
⌘-Right arrow	Go to next Terminal window
FN-Down arrow	Scroll down one screen at a time
FN-Up arrow	Scroll up one screen at a time
⌘-N	Open new Terminal window
Shift-⌘-N	Issue command in a new Terminal window
⌘-T	Open the Font panel so you can change the Terminal's default font settings, including the font family, size, and color

Command-Line Editing with tcsh

Mac OS X's default shell, *tcsh*, lets you move your cursor around in the command line, editing the line as you type.

There are two main modes for editing the command line, based on the two most commonly used text editors: Emacs and vi. Emacs mode is the default; you can switch between the modes with:

```
bindkey -e
```
    Select Emacs bindings

```
bindkey -v
```
    Select vi bindings

The main difference between the Emacs and vi bindings is that the Emacs bindings are modeless (i.e., they always work). With the vi bindings, you must switch between insert and command modes; different commands are useful in each mode. Additionally:

- Emacs mode is simpler; vi mode allows finer control.
- Emacs mode allows you to cut text and set a mark; vi mode does not.
- The command-history-searching capabilities differ.

Emacs Mode

Tables 8 through 10 describe the various editing keystrokes available in Emacs mode.

Table 8. Cursor-positioning commands (Emacs mode)

Command	Description
Control-B	Move the cursor back (left) one character
Control-F	Move the cursor forward (right) one character
Esc-B	Move the cursor back one word
Esc-F	Move the cursor forward one word
Control-A	Move the cursor to the beginning of the line
Control-E	Move the cursor to the end of the line

Table 9. Text-deletion commands (Emacs mode)

Command	Description
Del Control-H	Delete the character to the left of the cursor
Control-D	Delete the character under the cursor
Esc-D	Delete the next word
Esc-Delete or Esc-Control-H	Delete the previous word
Control-K	Delete from the cursor to the end of the line
Control-U	Delete the entire line

Table 10. Command control (Emacs mode)

Command	Description
Control-P	Recall the previous command from history
Control-N	Recall the next command from history
Up arrow	Recall the previous command from history
Down arrow	Recall the next command from history
cmd-fragment Esc-P	Search history for *cmd-fragment*, which must be the beginning of a command
cmd-fragment Esc-N	Like Esc-P, but search forward in the history
Esc *num*	Repeat the next command *num* times
Control-Y	Yank the previously deleted string

vi Mode

vi mode has two submodes: insert mode and command mode. The default mode is insert. You can toggle between the modes by pressing Esc; alternatively, in command mode, typing **a** (append) or **i** (insert) will return you to insert mode.

Tables 11 through 17 describe the editing keystrokes available in vi mode.

Table 11. Commands available (vi's Insert and Command mode)

Command	Description
Control-P	Recall the previous command from history
Control-N	Recall the next command from history
Up arrow	Recall the previous command from history
Down arrow	Recall the next command from history

Table 12. Editing commands (vi Insert mode)

Command	Description
Control-B	Move the cursor back (left) one character
Control-F	Move the cursor forward (right) one character
Control-A	Move the cursor to the beginning of the line
Control-E	Move the cursor to the end of the line
Delete or Control-H	Delete the character to the left of the cursor
Control-W	Delete the previous word
Control-U	Delete from the beginning of the line to the cursor
Control-K	Delete from the cursor to the end of the line

Table 13. Cursor-positioning commands (vi Command mode)

Command	Description
h or Control-H	Move the cursor back (left) one character
l or Space	Move the cursor forward (right) one word
w	Move the cursor forward (right) one word
b	Move the cursor back (left) one word
e	Move the cursor to the ending of the next word
W, B, E	Like w, b, and e, but treat whitespace as a word separator instead of any nonalphanumeric character
^ or Control-A	Move the cursor to the beginning of the line (first nonwhitespace character)
0	Move the cursor to the beginning of the line
$ or Control-E	Move the cursor to the end of the line

Table 14. Text-insertion commands (vi Command mode)

Command	Description
a	Append new text after the cursor until Esc is pressed
i	Insert new text before the cursor until Esc is pressed
A	Append new text after the end of the line until Esc is pressed
I	Insert new text before the beginning of the line until Esc is pressed

Table 15. Text-deletion commands (vi Command mode)

Command	Description
x	Delete the character under the cursor
X or Delete	Delete the character to the left of the cursor
d*m*	Delete from the cursor to the end of motion command *m*
D	Same as d$
Control-W	Delete the previous word
Control-U	Delete from the beginning of the line up to the cursor
Control-K	Delete from the cursor to the end of the line

Table 16. Text-replacement commands (vi Command mode)

Command	Description
c*m*	Change the characters from the cursor to the end of motion command *m* until Esc is pressed
C	Same as c$
r*c*	Replace the character under the cursor with the character *c*
R	Replace multiple characters until Esc is pressed
s	Substitute the character under the cursor with the characters typed until Esc is pressed

Table 17. Character-seeking motion commands (vi Command mode)

Command	Description
f*c*	Move the cursor to the next instance of *c* in the line
F*c*	Move the cursor to the previous instance of *c* in the line

Table 17. Character-seeking motion commands
(vi Command mode) (continued)

Command	Description
t*c*	Move the cursor just after the next instance of *c* in the line
T*c*	Move the cursor just after the previous instance of *c* in the line
;	Repeat the previous *f* or *F* command
,	Repeat the previous *f* or *F* command in the opposite direction

Additional Command-Line Keys

As was just illustrated, the *tcsh* shell offers dozens of special keystroke characters for navigation on the command line. Table 18 lists some additional command-line keys for use in either Emacs or vi editing mode.

Table 18. Additional key commands for the tcsh shell

Key command	Description
Control-C	Interrupt the process; cancels the previous command (⌘-. works as well).
Control-D	Used to signal end of input for some programs and return you to the shell prompt. If Control-D is issued at a shell prompt, it will close the Terminal window.
Control-I	Display an *ls*-style listing of a directory's contents; directories in the output will have a forward slash (/) after the directory name.
Control-J	Same as pressing the Return (or Enter) key; hitting Control-J after issuing a command will invoke the command, or it will take you to the next line in the shell if no command was given.
Control-K	Remove everything to the right of the insertion point.
Control-L	Clear the display.
Control-Q	Restart output after a pause by Control-S.
Control-S	Pause the output from a program that's writing to the screen.
Control-T	Transpose the previous two characters.
Control-Z	Suspend a process. To restart the process, issue the *bg* or *fg* command to place the process in the background or foreground, respectively.

Table 18. Additional key commands for the tcsh shell (continued)

Key command	Description
Esc-C	Capitalize the word following the insertion point.
Esc-Esc	If only a partial path or filename is entered, pressing the Esc key twice will complete the name.
Esc-L	Change the next word to all lowercase letters.
Esc-U	Change the next word to all uppercase letters.
Tab	Has the same effect as pressing the Esc key twice.

Additional Shell Commands

One of the first things that traditional Unix users will notice when they start poking around in the Terminal is that there are a few new commands they'll need to add to their repertoire. Three that we'll discuss here are *bindkey*, *defaults*, and *open*.

bindkey

bindkey is a *tcsh* shell command, used to select, examine, and define key bindings for use in the Terminal. Table 19 shows the various uses of the *bindkey* command.

Table 19. Using the bindkey command

Command	Description
bindkey	List all of the key bindings
bindkey -c key cmd	Bind *key* to Unix command *cmd*
bindkey -d	Restore the default key bindings
bindkey -e	Change the key bindings to Emacs mode
bindkey key	List the bindings for *key*
bindkey key cmd	Bind *key* to editing command *cmd*
bindkey -l	List the editing commands and their meanings
bindkey -r key	Remove binding for *key*
bindkey -s key str	Bind *key* to string *str*

Table 19. Using the bindkey command (continued)

Command	Description
bindkey -u	Display a message, showing how to use the *bindkey* command
bindkey -v	Change the key bindings to vi mode

For additional information on key bindings and how to alter them, see *Using csh & tcsh* (O'Reilly & Associates, Inc., 1995).

defaults

When you customize your Mac using the System Preferences, all of those changes and settings are stored in what's known as the defaults system. Everything that you've done to make your Mac yours is stored as XML data in the form of a *property list* (or *plist*). Your property lists are stored in *~/Library/Preferences*.

WARNING

Using the *defaults* command is not for the foolhardy. If you're not comfortable with the command line or unsure of how to change a setting properly, you should stick to using the application's Preferences pane, rather than trying to use the *defaults* command.

If you do manage to mangle your settings, the easiest way to correct the problem is to go back to that application's Preferences pane and reset your preferences.

Every time you change one of those settings, that particular property list is updated. For the initiated, there are two other ways to alter the property lists. The first is by using the PropertyListEditor application (*/Developer/Applications*), and the other is by using the *defaults* command in the Terminal. Extensive coverage of both is beyond the scope of this book, but we'll show you a basic example of how to use the *defaults* command.

Examples

The following are some examples of working with the *defaults* command:

View all of the user defaults on your system
```
% defaults domains
```

This will print a listing of all of the *domains* in the user's defaults system. The list you'll see are run together with spaces in between—not quite the prettiest way to view them.

View the settings for your Terminal
```
% defaults read com.apple.Terminal
```

This command reads the settings from the *com.apple. Terminal.plist* file, found in *~/Library/Preferences*. This listing is rather long, so you might want to pipe the output to *less* or *more* to view the contents one screen at a time:

```
% defaults read com.apple.Terminal | more
```

Change your Terminal's opaqueness so you can see through it
Near the end of that listing, look for the following:

```
TerminalOpaqueness = 1.00;
```

You'll see that it's value is set to 1.00, or 100%—a non-see-through Terminal. To change that setting, try the following:

```
% defaults write com.apple.Terminal ↵
TerminalOpaqueness 0.75
```

After a short pause, you'll be returned to another command prompt. Enter *exit*, and close that Terminal window, then open a new Terminal window to see your new semitransparent window. The value we've given sets the opaqueness to 75%.

For additional options and to learn more about how to use the *defaults* command, enter *defaults -help* or view the defaults manpage (*man defaults*).

open

With Mac OS X, you can launch any application from the command line using the *open* command. There are three ways to invoke the command:

open [*filename*]

> This will open the file and its associated application if it isn't already running. For example:
>
> ```
> % open textFile.txt
> ```
>
> would open the file *textFile.txt* using the default text editor, which is TextEdit.

open -a [*application_path*] [*filename*]

> The *-a* option lets you specify the application to use when opening the file. For example, let's say you have both Microsoft Office 2001 and Office v.X on your system and you want to open a Word file using Word 2001. If you use *open filename*, Word v.X will launch. To open the file with Word 2001, you need to do the following:
>
> ```
> % open -a /Volumes/Mac\ OS\ 9.2.2/Applications\ ↵
> \(Mac\ OS\ 9\)/Microsoft\ Office\ 2001/Microsoft\ ↵
> Word ~/Documents/filename.doc
> ```
>
> While that might look ugly (and it is), the command does work. In this case, Classic would also launch because Word 2001 is a Classic app.

TIP

There is a shortcut for inserting long pathnames like the one shown in this example: locate the application in the Finder, and drag the application icon from the Finder window to the Terminal window after typing *open -a* at the command line. The path for the application will be inserted after the command, and then all you need to do is tack on the path and filename for the file.

```
open -e [filename_path]
```
This will open the file using the TextEdit application. For example:

```
% open -e ~/Books/Templates/proposal_template.txt
```

Some additional examples of using the Terminal to open files and launch applications are shown here:

Open an HTML page using a browser other than Internet Explorer?

The other way to do this is to specify the application, using the -*a* option:

```
% open -a /Applications/Mozilla/Mozilla.app ↵
Public/mypage.html
```

The -*a* option is used to launch Mozilla (assuming you have Mozilla installed on your system, *http://www. mozilla.org*) for viewing *mypage.html*, located in your Public folder.

Launch Classic from the Terminal?

If you find that you're using the Classic environment, one way you can launch Classic from the Terminal is with the following:

```
% open /System/Library/CoreServices/Classic\ ↵
Startup.app
```

And while that does the trick, a faster way to do this is to set up an *alias* in the shell. To do this, enter the following on the command line:

```
% alias classic 'open -a /System/Library/ ↵
CoreServices/ Classic\ Startup.app'
```

Now all you need to do to launch the Classic environment is to type *classic* on the command line and hit return.

This assumes you're running *tcsh* as the default shell. If you're running *bash*, use the following to set up the *classic* alias:

```
$ alias classic='open -a /System/Library/ ↵
CoreServices/Classic\ Startup.app'
```

Basic Unix Commands

If you've never used Unix before, this section will serve as a quick introduction to issuing Unix commands from the Terminal. Experienced Unix users can probably skip over this section. For each of the following, you will need to be using the Terminal application. The commands you need to type are shown in bold.

View a command's description and its options?

All of the Unix commands on your system have a manual page (or *manpage* for short). To view the manpage for any command, you use the *man* command:

```
[localhost:~] chuck% man pwd
```

The instructions for using the *pwd* command (described next) is then displayed one screen at a time. If there is more than one screen for a command's description, you will see a percentage at the lower-left corner of the Terminal window telling you how much of the manpage has been viewed. To scroll to the next screen, hit the spacebar; you will be returned to the command prompt when you've reached the end of the manpage. The *man* command even has its own manpage, which can be viewed by using:

```
[localhost:~] chuck% man man
```

Where am I?

Type *pwd* on the command line, and hit Return; this will tell you the present working directory.

```
[localhost:~] chuck% pwd
/Users/chuck
[localhost:~] chuck%
```

Change directories?

Use the *cd* command:

```
[localhost:~] chuck% cd /Applications
[localhost:/Applications] chuck%
```

Go back a directory?

Use the *cd* command followed by two dots:

```
[localhost:/Applications] chuck% cd ..
[localhost:~] chuck%
```

Return to where you were before the last cd command?

Use the *cd* command followed by a hyphen:

```
[localhost:/] chuck% cd -
[localhost:/Applications] chuck%
```

Go back one or more directories?

Use the *cd* command with two dots and a slash (../) for each directory you want to go back. For example, to go back two directories:

```
[localhost:/Applications/Utilities] chuck% cd ../..
[localhost:/] chuck%
```

List a directory's contents?

This is accomplished using the *ls* command (see Figure 10).

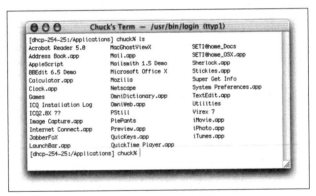

Figure 10. Listing a directory's contents with ls

By itself, the *ls* command creates a horizontal list of a directory's contents. Add the *-l* option to create a vertical list of a directory's contents, which also reveals more details about the file, directory, or application (see Figure 11).

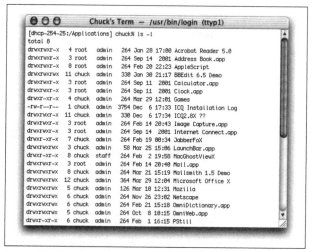

Figure 11. Listing a directory's contents using ls -l

To list all of the contents for a directory, including the dot files (described earlier), add the *-a* option (either with or without the *l* option) (see Figure 12).

When you issue a command like *ls -la*, the contents of some directories will scroll up, and you won't be able to see everything. One solution to this is to just issue the command and then use the Terminal window's scrollbar to go back up. Or, more efficiently, pipe (|) the command to *more*, which will display the contents of the directory one screen at a time (see Figure 13).

The word *more* will be highlighted at the bottom of the screen. To go to the next screen, hit the spacebar; continue doing so until you've found the item you're looking for or until you've reached the end.

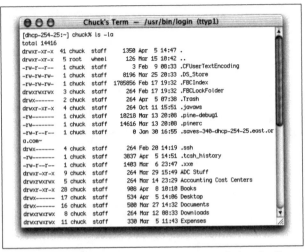

```
000          Chuck's Term — /usr/bin/login (ttyp1)
[dhcp-254-25:~] chuck% ls -la
total 14416
drwxr-xr-x  41 chuck  staff      1350 Apr  5 14:47 .
drwxr-xr-x   5 root   wheel       126 Mar 15 10:42 ..
-rw-r--r--   1 chuck  staff         3 Feb  9 00:33 .CFUserTextEncoding
-rw-rw-rw-   1 chuck  staff      8196 Mar 25 20:33 .DS_Store
-rw-rw-rw-   1 chuck  staff   1785856 Feb 17 19:32 .FBCIndex
drwxrwxrwx   3 chuck  staff       264 Feb 17 19:32 .FBCLockFolder
drwx------   2 chuck  staff       264 Apr  5 07:38 .Trash
drwxr-xr-x   4 chuck  staff       264 Oct 11 15:51 .javaws
-rw-------   1 chuck  staff     10218 Mar 13 20:08 .pine-debug1
-rw-------   1 chuck  staff     14616 Mar 13 20:08 .pinerc
-rw-r--r--   1 chuck  staff         0 Jan 30 16:55 .saves-340-dhcp-254-25.east.or
a.com~
drwx------   4 chuck  staff       264 Feb 20 14:19 .ssh
-rw-------   1 chuck  staff      3837 Apr  5 14:51 .tcsh_history
-rw-r--r--   1 chuck  staff      1403 Mar  6 23:47 .xxe
drwxr-xr-x   9 chuck  staff       264 Mar 29 15:49 ADC Stuff
drwxrwxrwx   5 chuck  staff       264 Mar 14 23:29 Accounting Cost Centers
drwxr-xr-x  28 chuck  staff       900 Apr  8 10:10 Books
drwx------  17 chuck  staff       534 Apr  5 14:06 Desktop
drwx------  16 chuck  staff       500 Mar 27 14:32 Documents
drwxrwxrwx   8 chuck  staff       264 Mar 12 08:33 Downloads
drwxrwxrwx  11 chuck  staff       330 Mar  5 11:43 Expenses
```

Figure 12. Listing all of a directory's contents—including dot files—using ls -la

How can I get a listing of a directory's contents without seeing the permissions?

Use *ls -l* and pipe the output of that listing to the *colrm* (column remove) command, as follows:

```
[localhost:/Applications] chuck% ls -l | colrm 1 47

Acrobat Reader 5.0
Address Book.app
AppleScript
BBEdit 6.5 Demo
Calculator.app
Clock.app
Games
ICQ Installation Log
ICQ2.8X ƒ
Image Capture.app
    .
    .
    .
```

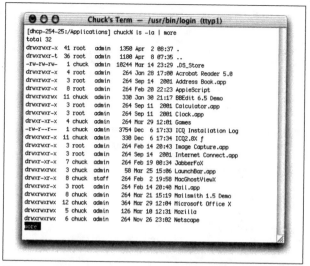

Figure 13. Listing a directory's contents with some assistance from the more command

The numbers following *colrm* (1 and 47) are used by the command to specify a range of columns to remove. (A column in the Unix world is a single character. In this example, the column range of 1 through 47—all of the characters preceding the file or directory name—will be deleted.)

Clear the display?

When you issue the *clear* command, the Terminal window will scroll down, placing the command prompt at the top of the display.

```
[localhost:/Applications] chuck% clear
```

You can also use Control-L to clear the display, and if you want to reset the Terminal window, use ⌘-K to clear the window's scrollback.

Create a new directory (or folder)?

Use the *mkdir* command, followed by the name of the new directory you'd like to create:

```
[localhost:~] chuck% mkdir NewDirectory
```

Remove an empty directory?

Use the *rmdir* command:

```
[localhost:~] chuck% rmdir NewDirectory
```

Remove a directory and all of its contents, including subdirectories?

Use the *rm* command with the *-rf* option to force the removal of the directory and its contents:

```
[localhost:~] chuck% rm -rf NewDirectory
```

Notice that this command will not prompt you before it deletes everything in the *NewDirectory* directory. You should use the *rm -rf* command with extreme caution.

Create an empty file?

There are many ways you can do this, but one of the easiest is by using the *touch* command:

```
[localhost:~] chuck% touch myfile.txt
```

Copy a file or directory?

Use the *cp* command:

```
[localhost:~] chuck% cp myfile.txt myfile2.txt
```

This will make a copy of *myfile.txt* and create *myfile2.txt* within the same directory. If you wanted to copy a file and place it in another directory, use the following:

```
[localhost:~] chuck% cp myfile.txt Books/myfile.txt
```

This will make a copy of *myfile.txt* and place that copy in the */Books* directory.

Rename a file or directory?

To rename a file, use the *mv* command:

```
[localhost:~] chuck% mv myfile.txt myFile.txt
```

This will rename the file *myfile.txt* to *myFile.txt* in the same directory.

Move a file or directory?

The following will move the file *myFile.txt* to the *Books* directory:

```
[localhost:~] chuck% mv myFile.txt Books
```

See what's inside a file?

For this, you can use either *cat*, *more*, or *less*:

```
[localhost:~/Books] chuck% cat myFile.txt
This is my file. I hope you like it.
Chuck
[localhost:~/Books] chuck%
```

Make a file or directory read-only?

For this, you'll need to use the *chmod* (change mode) command. Any one of the following will assign read-only permission to *myFile.txt* for everyone:

```
[localhost:~/Books] chuck% chmod =r myFile.txt
[localhost:~/Books] chuck% chmod 444 myFile.txt
[localhost:~/Books] chuck% chmod a-wx,a+r myFile.txt
```

The *chmod* command has many options; for more information, see its manpage (*man chmod*).

Compress a file?

To compress a file, you can use the Unix tape archive command, *tar*, as follows:

```
[localhost:~/Books] chuck% tar cvfz myFile.tar.gz ⏎
myFile.txt
```

The options used are as follows:

c   Creates a new archive.

v   Verbose; this option prints the filenames onscreen as files that are added to or extracted from the archive.

f   Stores files in or extract files from an archive.

z   Uses *gzip* to zip, or compress, the archive.

View the contents of a tarball?

To peek inside a tarball to see the files it contains, use the *tar* command with the *tvfz* options:

```
[localhost:~/Books] chuck% tar tvfz myFile.tar.gz
-rw-r--r--  1 chuck  staff  44 Feb 16 21:10 myFile.txt
```

The *-t* option is used to print the names of the files inside the tarball.

Open a .tar file?

To unpack a tarball (*.tar*), use the following:

```
[localhost:~/Books] chuck% tar xvf myFile.tar ⏎
myFile.txt
```

The *-x* option is used to extract the contents of the tarball. This command will unpack the tarball and place its contents in the file *myFile.txt*.

If you receive a *.tgz* (or *.tar.gz*) file, that means the tarball has been compressed using *gzip*. To decompress that file, use the following command:

```
[localhost:~/Books] chuck% tar xvfz myFile.tgz ⏎
myFile.txt
```

The *-z* option tells the tar command that the file it will decompress has been *gzip*'d.

Log in as the superuser?

Some commands require you to be the superuser (or the *root* user) before they can be issued. Rather than logging out and then logging back in as *root*, you can issue the *su* command, followed by the superuser's password:

```
[localhost:~] chuck% su
Password: ********
[localhost:/Users/chuck] root#
```

Now you have ultimate power—use it with great care as you could damage or overwrite something vital. When you are finished, issue the *exit* command to go back to being a normal user:

```
[localhost:/Users/chuck] root# exit
exit
[localhost:~] chuck%
```

PART V

Task and Setting Index

This final section of the book shows you how to configure and administer your Mac OS X system using the System Preferences and the Applications and Utilities that come with Mac OS X.

The book wraps up with a table that lists the special characters you can create from the keyboard.

Task and Setting Index

After rooting through all of the System Preferences and looking at the Applications and Utilities that come with Mac OS X, you'll quickly find that there are literally hundreds of ways to configure the settings for your system. In some cases, we've provided instructions for how to perform tasks using the GUI tools and by issuing Unix commands in the Terminal. Which is faster or easier to use is up to you to decide (but you're likely to realize quickly that the power of Unix is unmatchable by most GUI tools).

This section provides shorthand instructions to help you configure and use your Mac OS X system as quickly as possible. Each task is presented as the answer to a "How do I..." question (e.g., How do I change the color depth of my display?), followed by the shorthand way to execute the answer (e.g., System Preferences → Display). We've divided the tasks into the following ten categories:

Customizing the System
Files and Folders
Fonts and Font Management
Searching for and Locating Files
Obtaining Information About the System
Internet, Web, and Email
Modems and Dial-Up Networking
Networking
Printer Configuration and Printing
Maintenance and Troubleshooting

If you're new to Mac OS X, or if you just want to jog your memory when you can't quite remember where a particular setting is located, then this is the place to start.

Customizing the System

The following are options you can use to customize your system:

Change my desktop size/resolution, or the color depth of my display?
    System Preferences → Displays → Display panel

Change my Desktop image?
    System Preferences → Desktop

Use one of the Mac OS 9 background images for my desktop instead of the (boring) ones that come with Mac OS X?
    System Preferences → Desktop → Collection → Choose Folder. A Finder sheet will slide down; use this to navigate to Mac OS 9.2.2 → System Folder → Appearance → Desktop Pictures. Then select one of the following folders, and click the Open button: 3D Graphics, Convergency, Ensemble Photos, or Photos. The images in that directory will appear as part of your Desktop Collection.

Add a new background pattern, making it available to all users?
    Create or save the image to either the Abstract, Nature, or Solid Colors folder in */Library/Desktop Pictures*.

Change the double-click speed of my mouse?
System Preferences → Mouse → Mouse panel

Change the settings on my iBook's trackpad so it can emulate mouse clicks?
System Preferences → Mouse → Trackpad panel → Use trackpad for (Clicking, Dragging, Drag Lock)

Change my login password?
System Preferences → Users → Click on your username → Edit User → Password panel

From the command line, use the *passwd* command.

Change the date/time?
System Preferences → Date & Time → Date & Time panel

Specify how the date and time will appear in the menu bar?
System Preferences → Date & Time → Menu Bar Clock

Set my time zone?
System Preferences → Date & Time → Time Zone. A map of the world will appear; simply click and drag the time zone bar to your location on the map, and let go of the mouse. As you move the time zone bar, the date and time in the menu bar change dynamically.

Display the current date and time from the command line?
Use the *date* command:

```
[localhost:~] chuck% date
Sat Feb 23 16:33:43 EST 2002
```

Find out how long my system has been running?
Use the *uptime* command:

```
[localhost:~] chuck% uptime
 4:34PM  up 10:09, 2 users, load averages: 0.17, ⏎
0.33, 0.47
```

The *uptime* command displays, in the following order: the current time, how long the system has been running (*up 10:09*, or 10 hours 9 minutes), the number of users logged in to the system, and the load averages on the processor.

Change the name of my computer?
System Preferences → Sharing → File & Web panel. Enter the new name for your computer in the Computer Name text box.

Display the battery status for my PowerBook in the menu bar?
System Preferences → Energy Saver → Options panel; select the checkbox next to "Show battery status in menu bar."

Display a volume control in the menu bar?
System Preferences → Sound → Alerts → Show volume in menu bar

Automatically check for updates to the system?
System Preferences → Software Update. Check the radio button next to Automatically, then select the frequency (Daily, Weekly, Monthly) with which you would like the system to check for updates.

Have an application start up automatically after I log in?
System Preferences → Login → Login Items panel. Click the Add button, and then use the Finder to select the applications you would like to have started after you log in.

Adjust the amount of time my system needs to be idle before the screensaver kicks in?
System Preferences → Screen Saver → Activation

Quickly activate my screensaver when I know I'll be away from my desk for a while?
System Preferences → Screen Saver → Hot Corners. Mark a corner of the screen with a check mark to activate the screen saver when the mouse is moved to that corner. Likewise, you can place a minus sign in a Hot Corner to disable the screensaver when the mouse is moved there.

Protect my system from prying eyes while I'm away from my computer?
System Preferences → Screen Saver → Activation; select "Use my user account password" to require a password when waking the system from the screen saver.

Change the background of a window to a different color or to an image?
> Finder → View → as Icons, then use View → Show View Options (⌘-J); select either Color or Picture for the Background option.

Restart my computer automatically after a power failure?
> System Preferences → Energy Saver → Other Options

Enable full keyboard access so I can navigate through and select menu items without using a mouse?
> System Preferences → Keyboard → Full Keyboard Access

Files and Folders

The following are options for use with files and folders:

Create a new folder?
> Control-click → New Folder (in the Finder or on the Desktop)
>
> Shift-⌘-N

NOTE

In earlier versions of the Mac OS, ⌘-N was used to create new folders; now ⌘-N is used for opening a new Finder window.

Rename a file or folder?
> Click once on the icon, and then click once on the name of the file to highlight it (or press Enter). Type in the new name for the file or folder, and hit return to accept the new name.
>
> Click on the icon, and then use ⌘-I to open the Show Info window. Select Name & Extension from the pull-down menu, and enter the new file or directory name.

Change the program associated with a particular extension?
> Click on a file, and then use ⌘-I or File → Show Info. Select the pull-down menu, and go to "Open with

application." Click on the disclosure triangle of the application icon to reveal a list of applications that can open that file type; select one of the applications, or choose Other to select a different program. Once the application has been selected, click the Change All button to specify that application as the default for opening that file type.

Change the permissions for a file or directory?
Click on a file or directory, and then use ⌘-I or File → Show Info. Select the pull-down menu, and go to Privileges.

Use the *chmod* command. To learn more about *chmod* and its options, see its manpage (*man chmod*).

Copy a file to the desktop instead of moving it or creating a shortcut?
Select the file, then Option-click-drag the file to the Desktop (notice a plus sign will appear next to the pointer), and Release.

In the Finder, select the file → Edit → Copy → Home → double-click on the Desktop icon → Edit → Paste item.

Find out where an open document is saved on my system?
⌘-click on the name of the document in the title bar. A menu will drop down from the name of the file, showing you where the file is located. If you pull down to one of the folders in that menu and release the mouse, a Finder window will open for that location.

How can I create a disk image?
Applications → Utilities → Disk Copy → Image → New Blank Image (⌘-N). To create a disk image from an actual disk, such as your hard drive or a CD, choose Image → New Image from Device (Shift-⌘-I). Specify the details for the disk image and where you would like it to be saved; the image will be created and mounted on your desktop. Now just drag and drop items you included in the disk image, and Eject the image (⌘-E) to complete the process.

Display the contents of a shared folder on another volume in my network?

    Finder → *volume* → *folder*

From your home directory in the Terminal:

```
[localhost:~] chuck% ls -la /Volumes/volume/folder
```

Quickly create a directory and a set of numbered directories (such as for chapters in a book)?

```
[localhost:~] chuck% mkdir -p NewBook/ ⏎
{ch}{01,02,03,04,05}
[localhost:~] chuck% ls -F NewBook
ch01/ ch02/ ch03/ ch04/ ch05/
```

Try doing that in a GUI—you can't! After issuing the first command, *ls -F NewBook* is used to list the folders within the *NewBook* directory, which shows us that five separate subdirectories have been created.

Quickly delete a directory (and its subdirectories) without sending it to Trash?

```
[localhost:~] chuck% rm -rf work
```

Make the Trash stop asking me if I'm sure I want to delete every file?

    Finder → Preferences; uncheck the option next to "Show warning before emptying the Trash"

Empty the trash of locked items?

    Shift-Option-⌘-Delete. The addition of the Option key forces the deletion of the contents of Trash.

Insert the current time into a Word file?

    Shift-Control-T

Give a file or folder a custom icon?

    Open an image file, and copy it with ⌘-C. Select the icon → File → Show Info (or ⌘-I). Click once on the file icon in the Show Info window, then paste (⌘-V) in the new image.

The proper image size for an icon is 72 pixels square.

Fonts and Font Management

Use the following options for fonts and font management:

How can I share fonts with other users on my system?
> If you're the administrator, move the font from your */Home/Library/Fonts* folder to */Library/Fonts*.

Where can I store new fonts I've purchased or downloaded from the Internet?
> Save them to */Users/username/Library/Fonts* for your personal use, or to */Library/Fonts* to allow everyone on the system access to them.

Why aren't my bitmap fonts working?
> Mac OS X doesn't support bitmapped fonts—only TrueType, OpenType, and PostScript Level 1 fonts are supported by Mac OS X.

How can I make my Mac OS X fonts available in Classic Applications?
> Open two Finder windows. In Window #1, go to Mac OS 9 → System Folder → Fonts; in Window #2, go to Mac OS X → Library → Fonts. In Window #2, select all of the Fonts (⌘-A), then Option-drag the Mac OS X fonts into the Mac OS 9 Fonts folder in Window #1.

What does the .dfont extension mean on some of my Mac OS X fonts?
> The extension stands for "Data Fork TrueType Font." Basically, this just tells you that this is a TrueType font.

How can I turn off font antialiasing?
> You can't, but you can adjust the minimum font size to be affected by font smoothing in System Preferences → General → Turn off font smoothing for font sizes x and smaller.

How do I create a Font Collection?

In TextEdit, go to Format → Font → Font Panel (⌘-T), and select Edit Collection from the pull-down menu at the bottom of the window. The title on the window will change to "Font – Collections". Click on the plus sign (+) at the lower-left to add a new item in the Collections column; double-click on the name (New-1), and enter a different name (such as BookFonts), and hit return. Select a font in the All Families column, and then click on the << button to add that typeface to your Family column. When you've added all of the fonts, click on the Done button.

Where are my Font Collections stored, in case I want to share them with another user?

/Users/username/Library/FontCollections. If you want to share a collection, place a copy of the collection in the Shared folder. All font collections have a *.fcache* file extension.

Searching for and Locating Files

The following will help you search for and locate files:

Find a file when I don't know its name?

Sherlock → Custom → More Search Options

Automatically index my hard drive to allow for content-based searching?

Sherlock → Preferences → Indexing Options

NOTE

Sherlock does not index filenames—only the contents of files. However, you can still search for filenames.

Find a file when I can't remember where I saved it?

Use the *locate* command in the Terminal. However, you must first update the *locate* database as follows:

```
[localhost:~] chuck% cd /usr/libexec
[localhost:/usr/libexec] chuck% sudo ./locate.updatedb
```

If you haven't built the *locate* database yet, this command could take a few minutes to run; after which, you will be returned to the command line.

NOTE

The *locate.updatedb* command is executed weekly by default, as noted in the */etc/weekly* file. However, you might want to issue this command shortly after installing Mac OS X.

Now you can use the *locate* command:

```
[localhost:/usr/libexec] chuck% locate temp98.doc
/Users/chuck/Books/Templates/temp98.doc
[localhost:/usr/libexec] chuck%
```

In this example, we used *locate* to search for the file *temp98.doc*; in return, the command tells us in which directory it's located.

Obtaining Information About the System

Use the following if you need to obtain system information:

Find out how much disk space I have left?

Finder → Mac OS X → File → Show Info; select General Information from the pull-down menu.

Finder → Applications → Utilities → Apple System Profiler → Devices and Volumes panel.

Issue the *df -k* command in the Terminal, as shown in Figure 14.

This shows the amount of space Used and Avail(able) for each of the mounted drives or partitions. The / filesystem is that of Mac OS X, which on this system is at 96% capacity (compared to 34% for the partition that holds Mac OS 9.2.2). Note that the numbers shown in the

---

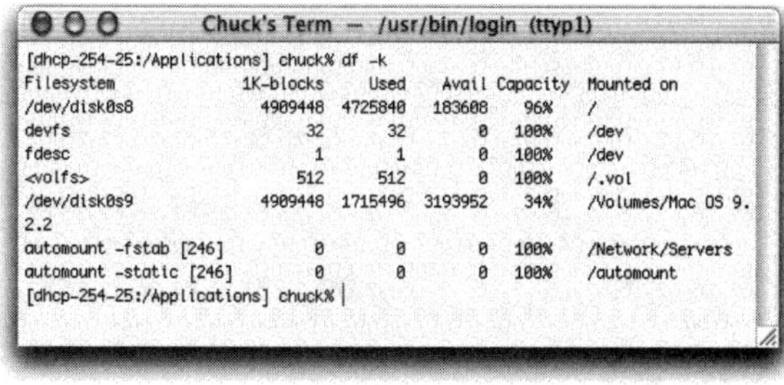

Figure 14. Using df -k to display the available disk space

Used and Avail columns are listed in kilobytes, so you'll have to do some quick math to figure out the size in megabytes. (The *-m* option, which would show the size in megabytes, isn't available.)

Find out how much memory I have?
→ About This Mac

Find out what version of Mac OS X I'm running?
→ About This Mac

Finder → Applications → Utilities → Apple System Profiler → System Profile panel. Look in the System overview section to see the exact build of Mac OS X.

Find out what version of Mac OS 9 I'm running?
In the Classic environment, use → Apple System Profiler → System Profile panel. Look in the System overview section.

Find out what processor my Mac has?
→ About This Mac

Finder → Applications → Utilities → Apple System Profiler → System Profile → Hardware Overview

What type of cache do I have and how big is it?
Applications → Utilities → Apple System Profiler → System Profile → Memory overview → Built-in memory

Find out whether a drive is formatted with HFS?

Applications → Utilities → Apple System Profiler → Devices & Volumes → Hard drive

Applications → Utilities → Disk Utility → Select the drive or partition → Information

Find out what programs (or processes) are running?

Finder → Applications → Utilities → ProcessViewer

From the command line, using the *ps -aux* command.

From the command line, using the *top* command.

Display the status of the computer's used and free memory?

Issuing the *top* command in the Terminal will show you something similar to what's shown in Figure 15.

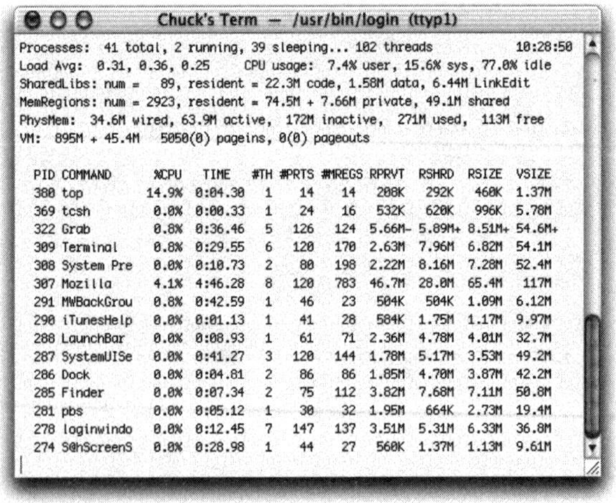

Figure 15. Display for the top command

The *top* command gives you a real-time view of the processes running on your system, as well as processor and memory usage. To see how much memory you have available, look at the end of the PhysMem line to see how much memory you have available; in this case, I can see that my system is using 271 megabytes (271M) of RAM and that I have 113 megabytes (113M) free. To stop the *top* command from running, hit Control-C or ⌘-. to cancel the process.

View the hardware connected to my system?

Finder → Applications → Utilities → Apple System Profiler. This information can be gathered from the System Profile and the Devices and Volumes panels.

Find the MAC (media access control) address for my Ethernet card?

Finder → Applications → Utilities → Apple System Profiler → System Profile panel. Look in the Network overview section.

System Preferences → Network → TCP/IP panel; toward the bottom of the window, look for a sequence of numbers and letters next to Ethernet Address.

Is there a quick way to gather information about my system?

Yes. To view the same information contained in your Apple System Profiler without the GUI, enter the *AppleSystemProfiler* command in the Terminal:

```
[localhost:~] chuck% AppleSystemProfiler

------- Apple System Profiler Tool v1.0.42 ----------

System version = Mac OS X 10.1.3 (5Q45)
Machine speed = 300 MHz
Bus speed = 67MHz
Customer serial number = Not available
Sales order number = Not available
L2 cache size = 1 MB
Machine name = PowerBook G3 series
boot device = 'PowerBook G3 series':Mac OS X
No memory information available
------ Ethernet -----
  Where = Built-in
  flags = =8863<UP,BROADCAST,b6,RUNNING,SIMPLEX, ↵
        MULTICAST>
```

```
   Ethernet address = 00.00.02.A7.B3.CB
   IP = 123.45.678.90
   netmask = 0xffff0000
   broadcast = 123.45.255.255
   ---------------
----- Slot information -----
Slot = E1
  Card type = display
  Card name = ATY,RageLTPro
  Card model= ATY,LT-C
  Vendor ID = 1002
  Device ID = 4c50
  ROM#      = 113-XXXXX-102
  Revision  = dc
Slot = PC Card A
  Card type = pccard
  Card name = pccard
  Card model= TXN,PCI1131-01
  Vendor ID = 104c
  Device ID = ac15
  ROM#      = Not available
  Revision  = 1
Slot = PC Card B
  Card type = pccard
  Card name = pccard
  Card model= TXN,PCI1131-01
  Vendor ID = 104c
  Device ID = ac15
  ROM#      = Not available
  Revision  = 1
No USB devices found
No FireWire devices found
---------------------
CD-ROM/DVD-ROM
  unit number = 0
  ata device type = atapi
  device serial =
  device revision = AC1b
  Product Identification = DVD-ROM SR-8182
  Vendor Identification = MATSHITA
Hard drive
Disk size = 9.36 GB (1K = 1024) 11 GB (1K = 1000)
  unit number = 0
  ata device type = ata
  device serial =                    163369
  device revision = 00X7A0C0
  device model = HITACHI_DK229A-10
```

```
Mac OS X
    Volume size = 4.68 GB (1K = 1024) 6 GB ⏎
    (1K = 1000)
    Ejectable = No
    Writable = Yes
Mac OS 9.2.2
    Volume size = 4.68 GB (1K = 1024) 6 GB ⏎
    (1K = 1000)
    Ejectable = No
    Writable = Yes
```

You could take this a step further and redirect the command's output to a text file, as so:

```
[localhost:~] chuck% AppleSystemProfiler > ⏎
sysprofile.txt
```

Now you can open, view, and print the file using TextEdit.

Internet, Web, and Email

Use the following settings as they relate to your Internet, web, and email usage:

Change the default email client and web browser from Mail and Internet Explorer, respectively?
　　To select a different email client, go to System Preferences → Internet → Email panel, and choose a different client in the Default Email Reader pull-down menu.

　　To select a different web browser, go to System Preferences → Internet → Web panel, and choose a different browser in the Default Web Browser pull-down menu.

Specify where files downloaded from the Internet will be saved?
　　System Preferences → Internet → Web panel. Click on the Select button next to the Download Files To text area.

Change my browser's default home page?
　　System Preferences → Internet → Web. Enter the new URL in the Home Page text box.

Set up an iTools account?

System Preferences → Internet → iTools → Sign Up. (You must be connected to the Internet to set up an iTools account.)

Turn on web sharing?

System Preferences → Sharing → File & Web → Web Sharing → Start. This will allow others to access your Sites folder (*/Users/username/Sites*) from the Internet. To learn more about Web Sharing, point your default browser to */Users/username/Sites/index.html*. The address for your personal web site will be: *http://yourIPAddress/~yourshortusername/*.

Register my copy of QuickTime Pro?

System Preferences → QuickTime → Registration

Listen to an Internet radio station?

Dock → iTunes → Radio Tuner. Clicking on the Radio Tuner option in the Source pane to the left, the right pane will change to show you a list of different music genres from which to choose. Click on the disclosure triangle next to a music type to reveal the available stations.

Use my own stylesheet for viewing web pages in Internet Explorer?

Internet Explorer → Explorer → Preferences → Web Browser → Web Content. Select the checkbox next to "Use my style sheet," then click on the Select Style Sheet button, then locate and select the Cascading Style Sheet (CSS) you want to apply.

Download a file via FTP?

If you've noticed, Mac OS X doesn't come with a graphical interface for FTP. There is a shareware version of the venerable Fetch program available (*http://www.fetchsoftworks.com*), but why bother paying for something when you can FTP files from the command line for free? For example, if you wanted to download O'Reilly's latest Word template for authors (stored in */pub/frame/templates/mswd*), you could use FTP from the Terminal as follows:

```
[localhost:~] chuck% ftp ftp.ora.com
Connected to tornado.east.ora.com.
<snip>
220 tornado.ora.com FTP server (Version wu-2.6.1(1)
Wed Aug 23 10:57:53 EDT 2000) ready.
Name (ftp.ora.com:chuck): anonymous
331 Guest login ok, send your complete e-mail address
as password.
Password: username@domain.com
230 Guest login ok, access restrictions apply.
Remote system type is UNIX.
Using binary mode to transfer files.
ftp> cd pub/frame/templates/mswd
250 CWD command successful.
ftp> ls
200 PORT command successful.
150 Opening ASCII mode data connection for /bin/ls.
total 1488
-rw-r--r--  1 61   81708 Jan 24  2001 temp.qreflet.rtf
-rw-r--r--  1 61   53775 Sep  1  2000 temp.rtf
-rw-r--r--  1 61  206848 Jan 24  2001 temp98.doc
-rw-r--r--  1 61   56801 Sep  1  2000 temp_med.rtf
-rw-r--r--  1 61   80714 Sep  1  2000 temp_prk.rtf
-rw-r--r--  1 61  196608 Sep  1  2000 temp_proc.doc
-rw-r--r--  1 61   60551 Sep  1  2000 temp_song.rtf
226 Transfer complete.
ftp> bin
200 Type set to I.
ftp> get temp98.doc
local: temp98.doc remote: temp98.doc
200 PORT command successful.
150 Opening BINARY mode data connection for temp98.doc
(206848 bytes).
226 Transfer complete.
206848 bytes received in 27.5 seconds (7514 bytes/s)
ftp> bye
221-You have transferred 206848 bytes in 1 files.
221 Goodbye.
[localhost:~] chuck%
```

The Word template (*temp98.doc*) will be saved in your home directory, as noted by the path ([localhost:~]). To learn more about using FTP from the command line, see *Learning Unix for Mac OS X* (O'Reilly & Associates, Inc., 2002).

Create shortcuts on my desktop for web sites I visit often, or for people I email frequently?

Open the TextEdit application, and enter a URL (such as *http://www.oreilly.com*) or an email address (such as *maxthekitty@mac.com*), then triple-click on the address to select the entire line and drag that to your desktop. This will create an icon on your desktop for whatever you drag there. When you double-click on the icon, your default web browser will open that URL, or your email client will create a new message window with the address specified by the shortcut.

You can take this a step further by adding these short-cuts to your Favorites folder (open the Finder and click on the Favorites heart icon in the toolbar, or press ⌘-T).

Set my computer to wake up from sleep mode when the modem rings?

System Preferences → Energy Saver → Options → Wake Options

Modems and Dial-Up Networking

Use the following options to configure your modem and dial-up networking:

Configure a modem for dialing into my ISP?

Go to System Preferences → Network, and follow these steps:

1. Select New Location from the Location pull-down menu. Enter a name for the new location (for example, My ISP), and click OK.

2. Select Internal Modem from the Show pull-down menu.

3. In the TCP/IP panel, select Using PPP from the Configure pull-down menu.

4. Fill in the blanks on the PPP panel.

5. Select your modem type from the Modem panel.

6. Click the Apply Now button.

Make sure my modem is working?
   Applications → Utilities → Internet Connect

Find out the speed of my dial-up connection?
   Applications → Utilities → Internet Connect. The bottom section of the window will tell you the speed of your connection.

Disable call-waiting on my phone when using the modem?
   System Preferences → Network → PPP. Insert *70 to the beginning of the telephone number you're dialing (e.g., *70, 1-707-555-1212).

Where are my modem configuration files stored?
   /Library/Modem Scripts

Specify how many times my modem will redial if it detects a busy signal?
   System Preferences → Network → Show → Internal Modem → PPP panel → PPP Options → Session Options

Networking

The following settings aid with networking options:

Configure my system to connect to an Ethernet network?
   Go to System Preferences → Network, and follow these steps:

1. Select New Location from the Location pull-down menu. Enter a name for the new location (for example, ORA-Local), and click OK.

2. Select Built-in Ethernet from the Show pull-down menu.

3. From the Configure pull-down menu in the TCP/IP panel, select Using DHCP if your IP address will be assigned dynamically, or Manually if your machine will have a fixed IP address. (In most cases, particularly if you have a broadband Internet connection at home, your IP address will be assigned via DHCP.)

4. If you're on an AppleTalk network, select the Make AppleTalk Active option in the AppleTalk panel, and select your Zone (if any).

5. Click the Apply Now button.

Configure my AirPort settings for wireless networking?
Follow the steps for connecting to an Ethernet network first, and then use Applications → Utilities → AirPort Setup Assistant. The settings you've applied for your regular network will be applied to your AirPort settings.

Find out the speed of my network connection?
Applications → Utilities → Network Utility → Info panel; look next to Link Speed in the Interface Information section.

Find out what's taking a site so long to respond?
Applications → Utilities → Network Utility → Ping panel; enter the network address for the location (e.g., *www.domain.com*, or *10.0.2.1*).

Use the *ping* command:

```
[localhost:~] chuck% ping hostname
```

Trace the route taken to connect to a web page?
Applications → Utilities → Network Utility → Traceroute panel; enter the URL for the location.

Use the *traceroute* command:

```
[localhost:~] chuck% traceroute hostname
```

Restrict access to my computer so others can get files I make available to them?

System Preferences → Sharing → File & Web panel. Click on the Start button in the File Sharing section to give others access to your Public folder (*/Users/username/Public*). The Public folder is read-only, which means that other people can only view or copy files from that directory; they cannot write files to it.

Where can my coworkers place files on my computer without getting access to the rest of my system?

With file sharing turned on, people can place files, folders, or even applications in your Drop Box, located within the Public folder (*/Users/username/Public/Drop Box*).

Quickly switch to an AirPort network after disconnecting the Ethernet cable from my iBook?

System Preferences → Network → Show → Active Network Ports. Click on the checkboxes next to the network ports you want to enable, and drag the ports in the list to place them in the order in which you're most likely to connect to them. (Of course choosing the Automatic location should do this for you, but it doesn't always work.)

View what's inside someone else's Public folder in their iTools iDisk?

Go → Connect to Server. At the bottom of the dialog box, type *http://idisk.mac.com/membername/Public*. Click Connect, or press Enter.

Connect to a networked drive?

Go → Connect to Server (⌘-K)

If the server to which you want to connect is part of your local area network (LAN), click on the Local Network icon in the left pane, and select the server name to the right. If the server you want to connect to is part of your local AppleTalk network, click on the AppleTalk Network icon in the left pane, and select the server or computer name to the right.

Connect to an SMB share?

If you need to connect to a Windows server, you will need to specify the Address in the text box as follows:

```
smb://hostname/sharename
```

After clicking the Connect button, you will be asked to supply the domain to which you wish to connect and your username and password.

NOTE

If you make a mistake, don't expect the error message to give you any assistance in figuring out why you weren't able to connect to the share.

You can speed up this process by supplying the domain and your username, as follows:

```
smb://domain;username@hostname/sharename
```

where *domain* is the NT domain name; *username* is the name you use to connect to that domain; and *hostname* and *sharename* are the server name and shared directory that you have or want access to. Now when you click on the Connect button, all you will need to enter is your password (if one is required), and the networked drive will appear on your desktop.

TIP

Before pressing the Connect button, press the Add to Favorites button first. This will save you time in the future if you frequently need to connect to the same drive, since you won't have to enter that address again.

Printer Configuration and Printing

Use the following options for printer configuration and printing:

Configure a printer?
> Applications → Utilities → Print Center → Add Printer →
> Select how the printer is connected using the pull-down
> menu (AppleTalk, LPR Printers using IP, USB, or via
> Directory Services):
>
> - If you selected AppleTalk, select the zone (if any)
>   using the second pull-down menu, choose the printer
>   in the lower pane, then click the Add button.
>
> - If you selected LPR Printers using IP, you will need to
>   know and fill in the IP address of the printer; select
>   the printer model, and click the Add button.
>
> - If you selected USB, select the name of the printer
>   and the printer model, then click the Add button.
>
> - If you selected Directory Services, select the printer
>   name, and then click the Add button.

View the jobs in the print queue?
> Applications → Utilities → Print Center → Double-click
> on the name of the printer to see the print queue

Cancel a print job?
> Applications → Utilities → Print Center → Double-click
> on the printer name → Click on the name of the print job
> → Click on the Delete button

Halt a print job?
> Applications → Utilities → Print Center → Double-click
> on the printer name → Click on the name of the print job
> → Click on the Hold button. (Click on the Resume but-
> ton to start the job where it left off.)

*Configure my system so I can print from the command line
using the Terminal?*
> To do this, you must first issue the cryptic *at_cho_prn*
> command with either the *sudo* command or as *root*:

```
[dhcp-123-45:~] chuck% sudo at_cho_prn
Password: ********
1  East_Ora_EtherTalk       2  West_Ora_EtherTalk

ZONE number (0 for current zone)? 1
Zone:East_Ora_EtherTalk
   1: 0002.83.9dtpenguin1:LaserWriter
   2: 0002.86.9d DODO1:LaserWriter
   3: 0002.82.9d Chicken1:LaserWriter
   4: 0002.08.9d Rheas1:LaserWriter
   5: 0002.85.9d weka1:LaserWriter

ITEM number (0 to make no selection)?5
Default printer is:weka1:LaserWriter@East_Ora_
EtherTalk
status: idle
[dhcp-123-45:~] chuck%
```

In the example shown here, I've specified *East_Ora_
EtherTalk* as my AppleTalk zone and *weka1* as my
default printer for printing from the command line.

View a list of available AppleTalk printers on my network?
    From the command line, use the *atlookup* command:

```
[dhcp-123-45:~] chuck% atlookup
Found 156 entries in zone East_Ora_EtherTalk
0002.82.08      Chicken1:SNMP Agent
0002.82.9e      Chicken1:HP LaserJet
0002.82.9c      Chicken1:HP Zoner Responder
0002.82.9d      Chicken1:LaserWriter
0002.86.9d      DODO1:LaserWriter
0002.86.08      DODO1:SNMP Agent
0002.86.9e      DODO1:HP LaserJet
0002.86.9a      DODO1:HP Zoner Responder
0002.06.08      Kiwi:SNMP Agent
0002.06.9e      Kiwi:HP LaserJet
0002.06.9c      Kiwi:HP Zoner Responder
0002.06.9d      Kiwi:LaserWriter
0003.84.80      MacChuck:Darwin
0002.85.08      weka1:SNMP Agent
0002.85.9d      weka1:LaserWriter
0002.85.9e      weka1:HP LaserJet
0002.85.9c      weka1:HP Zoner Responder
<snip>
```

Send a text file to a PostScript printer?

For this, use the *enscript* and *atprint* commands:

```
[dhcp-123-45:~/Desktop] chuck% enscript -p- ↵
textFile.txt | atprint
Looking for weka1:LaserWriter@East_Ora_EtherTalk.
Trying to connect to weka1:LaserWriter@East_Ora_
EtherTalk.
atprint: printing on weka1:LaserWriter@East_Ora_
EtherTalk.
[ 3 pages * 1 copy ] left in -
[dhcp-123-45:~/Desktop] chuck%
```

The *enscript* command is used to translate plain text into
PostScript so the file can be printed. The *atprint* command lets you stream any Unix output to an AppleTalk
printer. In this example, the commands are piped
together (using the standard Unix pipe, |), which for-
mats the file and sends it to the default AppleTalk
printer. Additional information about *enscript* and its
options can be found in its manpage (*man enscript*).

Send a PDF file to the printer (including USB printers)?

Use the *Print* command:

```
[localhost:~] chuck% Print ch24.pdf
```

If you have a PostScript printer, you can also use *Print* to send PostScript or text files to the printer. The *Print* command will automatically send a text file through *enscript* before sending it to the printer.

Maintenance and Troubleshooting

The following settings deal with maintenance and trouble-shooting issues:

Force quit an application that's stuck?

Option-⌘-Escape will open a window showing all of the running applications. Select the troublesome application, and click the Force Quit button.

Option-click the application's icon in the Dock. A pop-up window will appear next to the icon with the Force Quit option; move the mouse over and release on that option.

Applications → Utilities → ProcessViewer → Select the process that's causing the problem → Processes → Quit Process.

Restart my system when it's completely frozen?

Hold down the Shift-Option-⌘ keys, and press the Power-On button.

Turn on crash reporting so I can see why an application crashed?

Applications → Utilities → Console → Preferences → Crashes panel → Select both options. Now when an application crashes, the Console app will automatically launch and display the cause of the crash.

Where are crash logs kept?

If you've enabled crash logging, they will be stored in ~/Library/Logs.

Fix a disk that won't mount?

Applications → Utilities → Disk Utility → Select the disk that won't mount → First Aid.

Partition a new hard drive?

Applications → Utilities → Disk Utility → Select the new drive → Partition

Erase a CD-RW disc or hard drive?

Applications → Utilities → Disk Utility → Select the CD or disk → Erase

Create a RAID (redundant array of independent disks) for my system?

Applications → Utilities → Disk Utility → Select the drives → RAID

Access command-line mode and bypass Aqua?

There are three ways you can access the command-line interface:

- Hold down ⌘-S when starting up the system; this is known as single user mode.

- At the login window, type >*console* as the username, don't enter a password, and click on the Login button. This is known as multiuser mode and is just like being in the Terminal, except that your entire screen is the Terminal.

- From the Terminal, type *sudo shutdown now*, and hit Return; this also places you in single user mode.

When you've finished diagnosing your system, type *reboot*, and press Return to reboot your system into Aqua.

Rebuild Classic's desktop?

System Preferences → Classic → Advanced panel. There is no need to rebuild Mac OS X's desktop, so holding down Option-⌘ keys at startup is futile.

All of the icons on my system look funny. Is there an easy way to fix this problem?

Even though Mac OS X is more reliable than earlier versions of the Mac OS, icons and such can still go haywire. The quick fix for this problem is to delete the three "LS" files (*LSApplications*, *LSClaimedTypes*, and *LSSchemes*) in ~/Library/Preferences.

There is a question mark icon in the Dock. What is this?

A question mark icon in the Dock or in one of the toolbars means that the application, folder, or file that the original icon related to has been deleted from your system. Just drag the question mark icon away from the Dock or toolbar to make it disappear.

I have a dual-processor G4 machine. Can I see how efficiently the processors are distributing the workload?

Applications → Utilities → CPU Monitor. Each processor will have its own meter bar.

View a log of software updates?

System Preferences → Software Update → Show Log.

How do I connect an external monitor or projector to my PowerBook without restarting?

Select → Sleep to put your laptop to sleep, plug in and turn on the display, and then hit the Escape key to wake your system and the display. You can then use the Display System Preference (System Preferences → Display) to turn display mirroring on or off as needed.

Special Characters

Included with Mac OS X is the Key Caps application (*/Applications/Utilities*), which is a keyboard widget that allows you to see which character would be created by applying the Shift, Option, or Shift-Option keys to any key on the keyboard. Key Caps also allows you to copy and paste the character you create into another application, such as Microsoft Word.

While this might seem useful, it can be a hassle to launch another app just to create one character and copy and paste it into another program. Fortunately, one of the most little-known/-used features of the Mac OS is its ability to give you the same functionality within any application—making Key Caps unnecessary if you know what you're doing. Table 20 lists these special characters. Keep in mind that this doesn't work for all font types, and some fonts such as Symbol, Wingdings, and Zapf Dingbats create an entirely different set of characters or symbols. For example, to create the symbol for the Command key (⌘), you would need to switch the font to Wingdings and type a lowercase *z*.

Table 20. Special characters and their key mappings

Normal	Shift	Option	Shift-Option
1	!	¡	⁄
2	@	™	€
3	#	£	‹
4	$	¢	›
5	%	∞	fi
6	^	§	fl
7	&	¶	‡
8	*	•	°
9	(	ª	·
0	)	º	‚
`	~	Grave (`)a	`
(hyphen)	(underscore)	– (en-dash)	— (em-dash)
=	+	≠	±
[	{	"	"
]	}	'	'
\	|	«	»
;	:	…	Ú
'	"	æ	Æ
,	<	≤	¯
.	>	≥	˘

Table 20. Special characters and their key mappings (continued)

Normal	Shift	Option	Shift-Option
/	?	÷	¿
a	A	å	Å
b	B	∫	ı
c	C	ç	Ç
d	D	∂	Î
e	E	Acute (´)[a]	´
f	F	ƒ	Ï
g	G	©	˝
h	H	˙	Ó
i	I	Circumflex (ˆ)[a]	ˆ
j	J	Δ	Ô
k	K	˚	
l	L	¬	Ò
m	M	µ	Â
n	N	Tilde (˜)[a]	˜
o	O	ø	Ø
p	P	π	Π
q	Q	œ	Œ
r	R	®	‰
s	S	ß	∫
t	T	†	ˇ
u	U	Umlaut (¨)[a]	¨
v	V	√	◊
w	W	Σ	„
x	X	≈	˛
y	Y	¥	Á
z	Z	Ω	ˌ

[a] To apply this accent, you must press another key after invoking the Option-*key* command. See Table 21.

One thing you might have noticed in Table 20 is that when the Option key is used with certain letters, it doesn't necessarily create a special character right away—you need to press another character key to apply the accent. Unlike the other Option-key commands, when used with the ` (backtick), E, I, N, and U characters, you can create accented characters as shown in Table 21.

Table 21. Option-key commands for creating accented characters

Key	Option-`	Option-E	Option-I	Option-N	Option-U
a	à	á	â	ã	ä
Shift-A	À	Á	Â	Ã	Ä
e	è	é	ê	˜e	Ë
Shift-E	È	É	Ê	˜E	Ë
i	ì	í	î	˜i	ï
Shift-I	Ì	Í	Î	˜I	ï
o	ò	ó	ô	õ	ö
Shift-O	Ò	Ó	Ô	Õ	Ö
u	ù	ú	û	˜u	ü
Shift-U	Ù	Ú	Û	˜U	Ü

For example, to create the acute-accented e's in the word *résumé*, you would type Option-E, and then press the E key. If you wanted an uppercase acute-accented E (É), you would press Option-E then Shift-E. Try this out with various characters in different fonts to see what sort of characters you can create.

Index

We'd like to hear your suggestions for improving our indexes. Send email to
index@oreilly.com.